SOCIO-HISTORICAL EXAMINATION OF RELIGION AND MINISTRY:
A JOURNAL OF THE GLOBAL CENTER FOR RELIGIOUS RESEARCH

VOL. 4, NO. 2
WINTER 2022
SPECIAL ISSUE

Copyright © 2022

www.shermjournal.org

ISSN 2637-7519 (print)
ISSN 2637-7500 (online)
ISBN 978-1-959281-15-3 (print)
ISBN 978-1-959281-16-0 (eBook)

GCRR Press
1312 17th Street Suite 549
Denver, CO 80202
www.gcrr.org

Printed copies of this issue are available for purchase on the GCRR website at: www.gcrr.org/products

General Editor:
Darren M. Slade, PhD

I0105918

Socio-Historical Examination of Religion and Ministry (SHERM Journal) is a biannual (not-for-profit) peer-reviewed academic journal that publishes the latest social-scientific, historiographic, and ecclesiastic research on religious institutions and their ministerial practices. SHERM is dedicated to the critical and scholarly inquiry of historical and contemporary religious phenomena, both from within particular religious traditions and across cultural boundaries, so as to inform the broader socio-historical analysis of religion and its related fields of study.

The purpose of SHERM Journal is to provide a scholarly medium for the social-scientific study of religion where specialists can publish advanced studies on religious trends, theologies, rituals, philosophies, socio-political influences, or experimental and applied ministry research in the hopes of generating enthusiasm for the vocational and academic study of religion while fostering collegiality among religion specialists. Its mission is to provide academics, professionals, and nonspecialists with critical reflections and evidence-based insights into the socio-historical study of religion and, where appropriate, its implications for ministry and expressions of religiosity.

TABLE OF CONTENTS

VOL. 4, NO. 2
WINTER 2022
SPECIAL ISSUE

COUNTER APOLOGETICS

Evidence-Based Analysis of English Texts Written on Jesus' Resurrection

Michael J. Alter,
Independent Researcher

Abstract: *Since 2004, Gary Habermas has referenced his resurrection bibliography. Frequently, Habermas and Christian apologists assert that the scholarly consensus is that writers support the resurrection: a solid majority (about 75%) of scholars who have published books or articles on Jesus' resurrection accept the historicity of the empty tomb. However, Habermas has not presented supporting evidence for the past twenty years. This article collects and presents factual data and information about the authors of nonjuvenile, English-language texts, at least forty-eight pages written during the past 500 years on Jesus' resurrection. Significant categories of data investigated include (1) degree(s) earned and level of education, (2) occupation and interests, and (3) religion or denomination. Approximately 775 books (including six double-counted debates) were surveyed, with 713 pros and 62 contras. Pro authors were 610 and forty-six contras. The data substantiates and expands the earlier report by Alter and Slade. This article provides evidence that a remarkably high proportion of the English-language books written about Jesus' resurrection were by members of the clergy or people linked to seminaries and those having a professional and personal interest in the subject matter.*

Keywords: Resurrection, Gary R. Habermas, Minimal Facts, Historical Jesus, Apologetics

Introduction

In the past five centuries, over 700 English texts (non-juvenile), at least forty-eight pages, have been published about the resurrection of Jesus. Frequently, Christian apologists, commentators, and theologians present a common reframe that the *scholarly consensus* is that writers support the resurrection. Most notably, Gary R. Habermas claimed that a solid majority (about 75%) of *scholars* who have published books or articles on Jesus' resurrection accept the historicity of the empty tomb.[1] They cite a landmark 2005 article by Habermas as their evidentiary proof. In addition, afterward, Christian apologists, commentators, and theologians note a jointly published

---

[1] Habermas, "Resurrection from 1975 to the Present," 135–53.

Socio-Historical Examination of Religion and Ministry
Volume 4, Issue 2, Winter 2022 shermjournal.org
© Michael J. Alter
Permissions: editor@shermjournal.org
ISSN 2637-7519 (print), ISSN 2637-7500 (online)
https://doi.org/10.33929/sherm.2023.vol4.no2.01 (article)

GLOBAL
CENTER *for*
RELIGIOUS
RESEARCH
ACADEMIC INSTITUTE
GCRR

text by Habermas and Michael Licona: *The Case for the Resurrection of Jesus*.[2] In 2010, resurrection scholar Michael R. Licona published the highly acclaimed, modified version of his Ph.D. dissertation, *The Resurrection of Jesus: A New Historiographical Approach*. In Licona's introduction, he wrote, "Habermas has compiled a massive bibliography consisting of approximately 3,400 scholarly journal articles and books."[3] Two years later, Habermas published a widely influential article, particularly its allusion to a bibliography of 3400 sources.[4] Citations that mention Habermas's 3,400 references have appeared in various texts, journals, online articles, and podcasts.[5] Textual references include the works of Andrew Ter Ern Loke, Brian K. Morley, William A. Dembski and Michael R. Licona, Benjamin C. Shaw, and Robert B. Stewart.[6]

Surprisingly, an article by Michael Alter and Darren Slade reveals that if readers examine the authors who have published books in English on the topic of Jesus' resurrection, the seventy-five percent figure is, if anything, an underestimate.[7] Therefore, at first sight, this finding may seem to support the Christian apologist's claim of a solid scholarly consensus in favor of the empty tomb and Jesus' resurrection.

In 2021, Alter and Slade co-published "Dataset Analysis of English Texts Written on the Topic of Jesus' Resurrection: A Statistical Critique of Minimal Facts Apologetics." They confirmed, digging deeper; however, a different picture emerged. Their article "reveals that a remarkably high proportion of the English-language books written about Jesus' resurrection were by members of the clergy or people linked to seminaries. The data means any so-called scholarly consensus on the subject of Jesus' resurrection is wildly inflated due to a biased sample of authors who have a professional and personal interest in the subject matter."[8] Moreover, the data confirmed that *"Pro-Resurrection authors outnumber Contra-Resurrection authors by a factor of*

---

[2] Habermas and Michael Licona, *The Case for the Resurrection of Jesus*, 70

[3] Licona, *The Resurrection of Jesus*, 19.

[4] Habermas, "The Minimal Facts Approach to the Resurrection of Jesus," 18.

[5] Readers must note that Habermas's forthcoming text expands his working bibliography to about 4,500.

[6] See Loke, *Investigating the Resurrection of Jesus Christ*, *1*; Morley, *Mapping Apologetics*, *339n30;* Dembski and Licona, eds., *Evidence for God*, *177*; Shaw, "Philosophy of History, Historical Jesus Studies, and Miracles," 61–80; and Stewart, "On Habermas's Minimal Facts Argument," 1–14. In contrast, Michael J. Alter's forthcoming text, *The Resurrection and Its Apologetics Vol. 1* strongly challenges the Minimal Facts approach to Jesus' resurrection.

[7] Alter and Slade, "Dataset Analysis," 367.

[8] Alter and Slade, "Dataset Analysis," 368.

about twelve-to-one. (Italics added for emphasis) However, their article did not provide evidentiary proof substantiating its findings.

In other words, most books on the resurrection are by committed Christians. "We may legitimately presume that most of them already accepted the historicity of Jesus' resurrection long before they became scholars."[9] Indeed, apologist Gregory Koukl admits that most apologists first came to faith through personal experiences, not evidence.[10]

Frequently and sensibly, detractors and skeptics criticize Habermas because, during the past twenty years or so, he does *not* provide data supporting his claims. Alter's future text, *The Resurrection and Its Apologetics Volume 2*, devotes a section on that topic disputing the claim. A notable critic voicing equal concern is Richard Carrier.[11] Noteworthy, they and others seek to know who these people are who have written about the resurrection. More precisely, several questions include missing *minimal facts* about the authors: (1) level of education and degree of expertise (profession or layperson), (2) experience and professional service, and (3) religion or denomination.

Alter, in 2020 published, *A Thematic Access Oriented Bibliography on the Resurrection of Jesus's Resurrection*. That essential reference text organized more than 7,000 English sources into twelve main categories and subcategories, designed to help researchers find the most relevant literature quickly and efficiently. Returning to Alter and Slade, their abstract reads:

This article collects and examines data relating to the authors of English-language texts written and published during the past 500 years on the subject of Jesus' resurrection and then compares this data to Gary R. Habermas' 2005 and 2012 publication on the subject. To date, there has been no such inquiry. This present article identifies 735 texts spanning five centuries (from approximately 1500 to 2020). The data reveals 680 Pro-Resurrection books by 601 authors (204 by ministers, 146 by priests, 249

---

[9] This is, in fact, the case with apologist Gary Habermas, who regularly shares stories with his students about being a committed Christian in his youth long before obtaining a college degree. As fellow apologist John Frame once observed, "Habermas in the end presupposes a Christian view of evidence and probability" (Frame, "*A Presuppositionalist's Response*," 137). Quote from Alter and Slade, "Dataset Analysis," 368 n2.

[10] Koukl, *Tactics*, 55. Tony Campolo also confesses, "My apologetic, I explained, was determined by an a priori commitment. I believed first, then constructed arguments to support what I believed....In the end, isn't what we believe more highly contingent upon decisions we make rather than on empirical evidence?" (McLaren and Campolo, *Adventures in Missing the Point*, 108).

[11] Carrier, "Innumeracy: A Fault to Fix."

by people associated with seminaries, 70 by laypersons, and 22 by women). This article also reveals that a remarkably high proportion of the English-language books written about Jesus' resurrection were by members of the clergy or people linked to seminaries, which means any so-called scholarly consensus on the subject of Jesus' resurrection is wildly inflated due to a biased sample of authors who have a professional and personal interest in the subject matter. Pro-Resurrection authors outnumber Contra-Resurrection authors by a factor of about twelve-to-one. In contrast, the 55 Contra-Resurrection books, representing 7.48% of the total 735 books, were by 42 authors (28 having no relevant degrees at the time of publication). The 42 contra authors represent only 6.99% of all authors writing on the subject.[12]

Although the Alter-Slade article presented first-time data about the authors of 735 English texts on the resurrection, it lacked crucial information that researchers require. Like Habermas, it did not present supporting information about the 601 pro-resurrection and 42 con-resurrection authors. Those deficiencies require acknowledging and engaging. For example, in the abstract, they write that of the 680 Pro-Resurrection books by 601 authors, 204 were written by ministers, 146 by priests, and 249 by people associated with seminaries.[13]

Importantly, this article provides information about the authors' credibility and potential biases from both sides of the religious aisle, exposing the likelihood of a confirmation bias among credentialed *true believers* who conclude something they already believed: God raised Jesus from the dead.[14] This article engages and interacts with Habermas's claims and the deficiencies in the Alter-Slade article. Furthermore, it provides missing facts demanded by biblical scholars, detractors, and skeptics.

Aim of This Article

This article aims to collect and present factual data and information about the authors of English-language texts written and published during the past 500 years on Jesus' resurrection. Categories of data investigated include (1) degree(s) and level of education, (2) experience and occupation, (3) and religion

---

[12] Alter and Slade, "Dataset Analysis," 367.
[13] Alter and Slade, "Dataset Analysis," 367.
[14] Habermas discusses this topic in his forthcoming text (chapter 1, pages 15–27, "A Concept of History.")

or denomination. The text must be English, nonjuvenile, and at least forty-eight pages.[15]

This article employs several variables. They are visible in the seven-column spreadsheet seen in Table 1, 3, and 4.

1. The text number (first number) and author or editor book number (seen in parenthesis).[16]
2. Author or editor's name.
3. Name of the text.[17]
4. The year the text was published.
5. Identification of (a) the degree(s) earned by the author, (b) the specific discipline(s) that the degree(s) related to (e.g., apologetics, history, ministry, philosophy, religious studies, theology), (c) the institution obtained from, and (d) whether the author was a layperson.[18]
6. A brief overview of the author's (a) nationality, (b) occupation (e.g., bishop, evangelist, minister, priest, professor), (c) experience, professional service, and (d) interest are visible to inspect.
7. The author's denomination or religion. (see Table 1)

Table 1: Sample Spreadsheet Heading

Book (Author) #	Author Name	Text	Year	Degree(s)	Occupation	Religion
147 (133)	Craig, William Lane, and Gerd Lüdemann.	*Jesus' Resurrection: Fact or Figment?*	2000	Ph.D. in philosophy; Ph.D. in theology	Professor of Philosophy at Talbot School of Theology	Christian

---

[15] Readers must be mindful that the number of pages in a published text is misleading. Publishers employ varying fonts, the gutter (The gutter of a book is the blank space where the left and right pages meet), and the top and bottom margins (Margins are the blank spaces found between the content and the edge of the page.), and the size of the text (e.g., 8 X 11, 8 X 12, 5 X 8, 6 X 9).

[16] Craig's first identified text is the 147th text in Table 3 and he is the 133rd author.

[17] The texts are listed chronologically from current to oldest.

[18] Frequently, when information was lacking, column 5 provides only a general description or listing about where the author obtained an education (Seminary/College/University).

Review of the Literature

A *Southeastern Theological Review* (Summer 2012) journal issue devoted extensive pages to Jesus' resurrection. In one article, "The Minimal Facts Approach to the Resurrection of Jesus," Habermas further clarified and illuminated the nature of his research.

> From the outset of my studies, I argued that there were at least two major prerequisites for an occurrence to be designated as a Minimal Fact. Each event had to be established by more than adequate scholarly evidence, and usually by several critically-ascertained, independent lines of argumentation. *Additionally, the vast majority of contemporary scholars in relevant fields had to acknowledge the historicity of the occurrence* (italics added). Of the two criteria, I have always held that the first is by far the most crucial, especially since this initial requirement is the one that actually establishes the historicity of the event. Besides, the acclamation of scholarly opinion may be mistaken or it could change....

Habermas elaborates about an important phrase: "the vast majority." Synonymously, the phrase "virtually all scholars" appears in the literature, interviews, and podcasts. Notably, he writes, "At least when referencing the most important historical occurrences, I frequently think in terms of a *ninety-something percentile head-count* (italics added). " Habermas explains why this information is crucial: "No doubt, this is one of the reasons why the concept has gained some attention."

Next, he describes his catalog stating "My bibliography is presently at about 3400 sources and counting, published originally in French, German, or English." The bibliography includes

1. Skeptical to liberal to conservative spectrum
2. Well-known and obscure writers
3. Authors who did not have specialized scholarly credentials or peer-reviewed publications

Habermas estimates that "The result of all these years of study is a private manuscript of more than 600 pages." Afterward, he candidly acknowledges "Most of this material is unpublished, though I have released some of the results in essays that specifically attempt to provide overviews of some of these current academic positions.[19]

The reader will note that Habermas listed two criteria for designating an event relating to Jesus' death and resurrection as a minimal fact: (1) the event is well-evidenced (usually for several reasons), and (2) the event is generally believed to have occurred by at least 90% of "critical scholars." This article, similar to Alter and Slade, will take no issue with Habermas's first criterion, only with his second. Briefly stated Habermas's research fails to satisfy his second criterion. Further, the standard itself needs to be modified to distinguish between a scholar's pre-conceived beliefs about Jesus and their subsequent opinions from academic research.[20] Moreover, it requires inquiring, "Where's the beef?"

Lack of Details about Scholars

There are numerous unanswered questions about Habermas's list of scholars who accept the empty tomb. Habermas needs to provide his readers with substantive details about these scholars. The following questions about his claims require answers:

- What is Habermas's definition of a "critical scholar" or a "scholar"? He does not define or elaborate on the difference between these terms.
- Which and how many of these writers are scholars?
- Which and how many of these scholars are, respectively, from German, French, or English-speaking nations or elsewhere?
- Which and how many of these scholars are Christians, Evangelical Christians, Christian apologists, Jewish, Muslims, agnostics, or atheists?
- Which and how many of these writers were New Testament scholars, historians, philosophers, rabbis, imams, or laypeople?

---

[19] Habermas, "The Minimal Facts Approach to the Resurrection of Jesus," 16–18.

[20] Slade a former doctoral student of Habermas, in the Alter-Slade article, provides insight. He says, "Habermas himself has stated that being criticized for his obstinate ideological dogmatism is simply part of the persecution that all true Christians should expect. When confronted with the notion that the 'minimal facts' tactic can only compile data and that it is his religious ideology interpreting the data in favor of Christianity, Habermas agreed. He simply concluded that everyone engages in a confirmation bias (Habermas, "APOL 900," May 26, 2016). See Alter and Slade, "Data Set Analysis," 372n9.

- Which and how many of these scholars are qualified experts in relevant fields such as biblical studies or ancient history?
- Which and how many of these scholars signed letters promising they would *not* reject various tenets of their faith?
- Which and how many scholars are ministers, pastors, priests, vicars, seminary instructors, Christian apologists, or missionaries?
- Which and how many of these works are scholarly publications and peer-reviewed?

Investigative Obstacles, Presuppositions, and Methodology

Alter reexamined approximately 700 sources in subcategories 1 and 2.[21] Reexamination aimed to determine texts for removal from Alter's original lists. Added to the original lists were newly published texts, forthcoming publications, and discovered older sources.

Investigative Obstacles

Readers are reminded from the Alter-Slade article that an exhaustive list of *all* texts ever written about Jesus' resurrection would consist of sources written in all languages, in all locales, and at any time since the birth of Christianity. However, due to time constraints, geography, accessibility, and limited research resources, an alternative was required to narrow the search. Consequently, this investigation only incorporates a nearly complete dataset of nonjuvenile English-language texts, at least forty-eight pages, arranged in Pro-Resurrection (Table 3) and Contra-Resurrection (Table 4). These texts, in turn, are sorted into seven columns.

Another obstacle was whether to single-count texts that consist of debates (whether to list the book exclusively by the first name of the debater appearing in the text and that person's category: pro or contra.). Six books were debates. An alternative approach was adopted. It incorporates listing *both* debaters in their respective pro or contra position. Consequently, the total number of texts lacks exactitude.

---

[21] Alter, *A Thematic Access Oriented Bibliography.*

Organization

This article focuses on several variables for presentation to answer the crucial question: "Where's the beef?":

(1) Author's name;
(2) Year of the published work(s);
(3) Identification of (a) the degree(s) earned by the author, (b) the specific discipline(s) that the degree(s) related to (e.g., apologetics, history, ministry, philosophy), (c) the institution obtained from, and (d) whether the author was a layperson or a scholar;
(4) A brief overview of the author's (a) nationality, (b) religion, and (c) occupation (e.g., bishop, evangelist, minister, priest, professor), and
(5) The author's denomination or religion.

This information was primarily, although not exclusively, gathered through eight sources: (1) the book(s) written by the author; (2) the publisher; (3) the author's curriculum vitae; (4) published biographies; (5) encyclopedias; (6) the Library of Congress Name Authority File (NAF); (7) LinkedIn; and (8) obituary notices.

Inclusions and Exclusions

This study is limited to non-juvenile texts (at least forty-eight pages) written exclusively in English and penned primarily within the past five centuries.[22] It

---

[22] The search was limited deliberately to the English language for five major reasons. First, from Alter's 2021 text, a healthy amount of data from approximately 700 texts was easily accessible. In contrast, Habermas's total of 3,400 sources included journal articles. His forthcoming text (*On the Resurrection: Evidences*, p. 2) says resurrection bibliography "currently standing at some 4,500 sources." Second, Habermas has never provided data detailing precisely how many texts (not articles) he analyzed were exclusively English, meaning the number of non-English texts may not have been statistically significant. Third, it is noteworthy that Habermas said, "By far, the majority of publications on the subject of Jesus' death and resurrection have been written by North American authors"; thus, presumably in the English language. Of note, thirty-two pro and only four con books in Alter's bibliography were English translations from other languages. Fourth, if this study incorporated non-English texts, there would be the question of which languages would be subject to exclusion and for what reason. Significantly, including only French and German titles (as Habermas does) while *excluding Arabic would skew the data since Islam rejects the historicity of Jesus' crucifixion*. Moreover, it is noteworthy that Habermas excludes other languages like Korean, Chinese, and Spanish. How can he claim that "most scholars" agree on a minimal fact if "most" scholars are actually excluded from his list? Five,

excludes texts about the Christ Myth (Jesus never existed). It also excludes resurrection texts that focus on the spiritual and theological meaning of the presumed events. One additional limitation was incomplete information about several authors.[23]

This article divides the data findings into two main categories: Pro (Table 3) and Contra (Table 4). The purpose of this division is to facilitate the examination of the data. However, the existence of more nuanced groupings is acknowledged.

Alter and Slade, and this article also examines the religious denomination and clerical status. These variables continued to present numerous obstacles to arriving at an accurate tabulation. For example:

1. Several authors changed their denominational affiliation, while overall categorization was difficult, if not impossible, for others.
2. Some members of the clergy employed various terms for their occupation. Often, this fact made it impossible to determine their denomination accurately.

Who Counts as a Scholar?

To be categorized as a "scholar" in the field, at least two obvious problems exist.

1. What is the definition of *a critical scholar*?
2. What are the relevant credentials for qualifications?

What is Habermas's definition of a *critical scholar* or a *scholar*? He does not define or elaborate on the difference between these terms. In 2017, one reader asked Bart Ehrman, can biblical scholars be historians? He responded, "I would say that most biblical scholars in fact are not historians. But some are. It depends on what their interests and expertise are."[24] Habermas, in his forthcoming texts partially lends credence to Ehrman's opinion, "If a scholar has an accredited

---

although limited to the English language, this data is not of limited value because it exposes serious defects in Habermas's apologetic methodology. Of course, the implications of this study should be subject to further investigation. Specifically, future research should build on this paper and investigate findings in non-English language texts, as well as journal articles. Collectively, they would present researchers with deeper insight into the writers of texts on this critical topic.

[23] Readers must be cognizant of the subjectivity about categorizing, including, and excluding resurrection texts.

[24] Ehrman, "*Can Biblical Scholars Be Historians?*"

terminal degree in the area being discussed, that would most likely qualify them."[25]

Tim McGrew, Ph.D., Philosophy, Professor and Chairman of the Department of Philosophy at Western Michigan University, and Christian apologist says:

> An advanced degree is indirect evidence that you know what you are talking about. It is useful as far as it goes. But indirect evidence must give way in the presence of direct evidence. Show me that you know what you are talking about, and I don't care whether you have the degree. Show me that you *don't* know what you are talking about, and I don't care whether you have the degree.[26]

An example is Lydia McGrew, Tim's wife. She describes herself: "I am a wife, mother, emeritus home schooler and scholar … As a scholar, I'm an analytic philosopher with a fairly hefty publication record in such areas as testimony, independence, probability theory, etc. More recently my work has extended to New Testament studies."[27] Presumably, credentialed detractors might claim she is unqualified to write in apologetics, philosophy, or theology. Lydia McGrew has one of the sharpest minds in these disciplines and can probably dance circles around those touted credentialed with a Ph.D. It is best to examine her literary output. It speaks for itself.

Several examples of writers of texts, chapters in texts, journal articles, and blog posts illuminate this point.

1. Richard Swinburne earned a Ph.D. in Philosophy from Oxford.
2. Lee Strobel is the former award-winning legal editor of *The Chicago Tribune* and an honorary doctorate recipient.
3. Matthew McGrew earned a Ph.D. in Philosophy from Vanderbilt University.
4. Pamela Binnings Ewen earned a Juris Doctor in Law.
5. James Patrick Holding earned an M.A. in Library Science.

---

[25] Habermas, *On the Resurrection*, 3.

[26] Tim McGrew is quoted in this Facebook status from Lydia McGrew on June 25th 2021.https://www.facebook.com/lydiamcgrewauthor/posts/pfbid02Rh2Eu37V4MWjvH6cu6aB VXTavFkVcSqZbsmaNEWQqM1FknyPPV5PunCAhkzcyUCFl. Source, Evan Minton, "The Concept of the Credentialed Layman."

[27] McGrew, "About Me,"

6. Gilbert R. Lavoie earned an M.D. in Internal Medicine and Occupational Medicine.
7. James Warner Wallace was a former Homicide Detective.
8. Greg Laurie does not have any formal seminary training.

Readers must diligently examine the authors' credentials provided in Table 3 and Table 4. At first appearance, a significant number, from those on both sides of the religious aisle, appear to possess credentials. Are these writers qualified to write a text, chapter in a text, or journal article about the resurrection?

A Doctor of Divinity (D. Div.) is an honorary degree conferred upon select professionals who have demonstrated an outstanding commitment to ministry and theology. In other words, a doctorate in divinity differs from a degree one receives after taking a course of college classes and completing a dissertation. In contrast, some writers have a D.D. or Ph.D. in religion and theology attached to their names. Wikipedia cites an example:

Billy Graham, who received honorary Doctor of Divinity degrees from The King's College and the University of North Carolina at Chapel Hill was regularly addressed as "Dr. Graham", though his highest earned degree was a Bachelor of Arts degree in anthropology from Wheaton College.[28]

Detractors may, in humorous sarcasm, remind readers that the three letters of Ph.D. are an acronym:

1. Permanent head damage
2. Piled higher and deeper
3. Push here for dummies
4. Please hide dangerous
5. Probability hypothesis density

The crucial question is whether the D.D. (Doctor of Divinity) or Ph.D. qualifies writers to write a text about the resurrection. The reader must be the final judge.

Research by Alter (2020) and this article confirmed that several authors had a "doctorate," but the degree was an honorary title. Examples of non-degree authors include Horace M. Du Bose, Curtis Hutson, Greg Laurie, A.A. Lipscomb, Lee Strobel, and Warren Wiersbe. These writers are in good

---

[28] Wikipedia, "Doctor of Divinity."

company. For example, Lewis Sperry Chafer, founder and president of Dallas Theological Seminary and the author of his eight-volume *Systematic Theology*, only received three honorary degrees, one that he gave himself. Similarly, Joel Osteen, a celebrity American lay preacher, televangelist, and prominent figure associated with prosperity theology, did not receive a degree from a divinity school. Nevertheless, he has millions of followers and readers.

One realistic response is that the degree earned is irrelevant. What matters is whether the book is:

1. Truthful.
2. Factual (i.e., it presents facts, not "alternative facts").
3. It cites "substantial" peer-reviewed evidence supporting its findings and interpretations.
4. Engages and interacts with ideas, pros, and cons about the resurrection.
5. Presents a broad scope about the resurrection (discussing numerous topics, authors, agendas, dating, apologetics, controversial issues, and current discussion.).
6. Depth of insight and knowledge.
7. Can withstand critical analysis.
8. Frankly admits when it is presenting an argument from silence.

Data

Before, Alter and Slade provided a detailed analysis of English texts about the resurrection.[29] A reduced summary of this (Alter's) article follows. Note that *categories overlap. They do not add up to the total.* (see Table 2)

1. Number of Pro-Resurrection Books
2. Number of Pro-Resurrection Authors
3. Number of Contra-Resurrection Books
4. Number of Contra-Resurrection Authors

---

[29] Alter and Slade, "Dataset Analysis."

Table 2: Total Number of Books and Authors

Number of Pro-Resurrection Books	713
Number of Pro-Resurrection Authors	610
Number of Contra-Resurrection Books[30]	62
Number of Contra-Resurrection Authors	46
Total number of texts	$713 + 62 = 775$[31]
Total number of authors and editors	$610 + 46 = 656$

Table 3: Pro-Resurrection Authors and Texts

Book (Author) #	Author Name	Text	Year	Degree(s)	Occupation	Religion
1 (1)	Aldrich, J. K.	*A Critical Examination of the Question*	1882	None	Pastor	Congregational
2 (2)	Alkier, Stefan	*The Reality of the Resurrection*	2013	Ph.D.	Prof. of New Testament and Church History	Protestant
3 (3)	Allberry, Sam	*Lifted: Experiencing the Resurrection Life*	2012	Studied theology	Minister	Anglican

---

[30] Total does not include advocates of the Christ Myth. Readers are reminded that a degree of subjectivity is involved in identifying and categorizing respective authors and texts.

[31] Note that six texts were double counted because they were debates.

4 (4)	Allen, O. Wesley	*Preaching Resurrection*	2000	Ph.D.	Professor of Preaching	Methodist
5 (5)	Allison, Dale C.	*The Resurrection of Jesus: Apologetics, Polemics, History*	2021	Ph.D.	Professor	Presbyterian
6 (5)		*Resurrecting Jesus: The Earliest Christian Tradition*	2005			
7 (5)		*The End of the Ages Has Come*	1985			
8 (6)	Alsup, John E.	*The Post-Resurrection Appearance Stories*	1975	Princeton Theological and University of Hamburg and Munich	Professor Emeritus of New Testament Studies	Presbyterian
9 (7)	Almodovar, Nancy A.	*Nothing Else Matters: How the Resurrection of Jesus Changes Everything*	2022	Ph.D.	Professor of World Religions	Lutheran
10 (8)	Alumkal, Jacob Paxy	*Death and Resurrection of Jesus Christ Implied*	2014	Ph.D.	Priest	Catholic
11 (9)	Anderson, Donald Edward	*Joy Comes in the Morning*	1990	M.A. and D.Min.	Pastor	Protestant

12 (10)	Anderson, Kevin L.	*But God Raised Him from the Dead*	2006	Ph.D.	Professor of Bible and Theology	Protestant
13 (11)	Andrewes, Lancelot	*Two Sermons of the Resurrection*	1609 (1932 repr)	M.A.	Bishop of Winchester	Anglican
14 (12)	Ankerberg, John and John Weldon	*The Passion and the Empty Tomb*	2005	D.Min., M.A., and M.Div.	Television host	Baptist
15 (12)		*Knowing the Truth About the Resurrection*	1996			
16 (12)		*Do the Resurrection Accounts Conflict?*	1990			
17 (13)	Archer-Shepherd, E. H.	*The Nature and Evidence of the Resurrection of Christ*	1910	M.A.	Rector	Anglican
18 (14)	Armstrong, William Park	*The Place of the Resurrection Appearances of Jesus*	1912	D.D.	Minister	Presbyterian
19 (15)	Arraj, Jim	*The Bodily Resurrection of Jesus*	2007	D.Th.	Psychologist	Catholic

20 (16)	Atkins, J.D.	*The Doubt of the Apostles and the Resurrection Faith*	2019	Ph.D.	Assistant professor	Christian
21 (17)	Atkins, Peter	*Ascension*	2001	Merchant Taylors' School and Sidney Sussex College	Bishop	Anglican
22 (18)	Augsburge, Myron S.	*The Resurrection Life*	2005	A.B., Th.B., and M.Th.	Pastor	Mennonite
23 (19)	Austin, E. Lorraine. C.	*Earth's Greatest Day*	1980	—	Author	—
24 (20)	Avis, Paul D. L.	*The Resurrection of Jesus Christ*	1993	Ph.D.	Priest	Anglican
25 (21)	Bacchiocchi, Samuele	*The Time of the Crucifixion and the Resurrection*	1985	Ph.D.	Professor of Theology and Church History	Seventh-day Adventists
26 (22)	Bain, Andrew	*Passion and Resurrection Narratives*	2018		—	
27 (23)	Balsiger, David W. and Michael Minor	*The Case for Christ's Resurrection*	2007	B.A.	Film and TV producer	Protestant

28 (24)	Balthasar, Hans Urs von and Aidan Nichols	Mysterium Paschale	1990	Ph.D.	Theologian	Catholic
29 (25)	Banks, William L.	Three Days and Three Nights: The Case for a Wednesday Crucifixion Date	2005	D.D.	Professor	Baptist
30 (26)	Bannerman, James	Inspiration, the Infallible Truth and Divine Authority of the Holy Scriptures	1865	D.D.	Reverend	Presbyterian
31 (27)	Baring-Gould, S.	The Death and Resurrection of Jesus	1888	M.A.	Priest	Anglican
32 (28)	Barker, Margaret	The Risen Lord: The Jesus of History as the Christ of Faith	1996	D.D.	Preacher	Methodist
33 (29)	Barnett, Henry C.	The Evidence of the Resurrection of Jesus Christ	1921	Franklin College	Admitted to the Indiana bar in 1875	Protestant
34 (30)	Barnhouse, Donald Grey	The Cross Through the Open Tomb	1961	Biola Institute; University of Chicago; Princeton Theological Seminary	Preacher	Presbyterian
35 (31)	Barth, Markus and Verne H. Fletcher	Acquittal by Resurrection	1964	Ph.D.	Reformed theologian	Protestant

36 (32)	Bartlett, David Lyon	*Fact and Faith*	1975	Ph.D.	Professor	Baptist
37 (33)	Barton, John	*Love Unknown*	1990	Ph.D.	Deacon	Anglican
38 (34)	Barton, Stephen C., and Graham Stanton	*Resurrection: Essays in Honour of Leslie Houlden*	1994	Ph.D.	Priest	Anglican
39 (35)	Barton, William Eleazar, et al.	*His Last Week: The Story of the Passion and Resurrection*	1905	D.D.	Clergyman	Congregational
40 (36)	Bass, Justin W.	*The Bedrock of Christianity*	2020	Ph.D.	Pastor	Christian
40 (37)	Bast, David M.	*Easter Hope: How Jesus' Resurrection Changes Life*	1996	Hope College and Western Theological Seminary	President of Words of Hope	Protestant
41 (38)	Bayer, Hans F.	*Jesus' Predictions of Vindication and Resurrection*	1986	Ph.D.	Professor	Protestant
42 (39)	Beard, Arthur	*Bar-Jonah: The Son of the Resurrection*	1887	M.A.	Reverend	Anglican

43 (40)	Beasley-Murray, George Raymond	*The Resurrection of Jesus Christ*	1964	D.D.	Evangelical Christian	Baptist
44 (40)		*Christ Is Alive!*	1947			
45 (41)	Beasley-Murray, Paul	*The Message of the Resurrection: Christ is Risen!*	2001	Ph.D.	Minister	Baptist
46 (42)	Beck, W. David and Michael R. Licona	*Raised the Third Day*	2020	Ph.D.	Emeritus professor of philosophy	Christian
47 (43)	Belknap, Jeremy	*Dissertations on the Character, Death & Resurrection*	1795	D.D.	Clergyman	Congregational
48 (44)	Belser, Johannes Evangelist	*History of the Passion, Death, and Glorification of Our Saviour*	1929	University of Tübingen	Priest	Catholic
49 (45)	Benedict XVI, Pope	*Jesus of Nazareth. Holy Week*	2011	St. Michael Seminary, Ludwig-Maximilian University	Priest	Catholic
50 (46)	Benesch, Friedrich	*Easter*	1981	—	Scientist	Protestant

51 (47)	Benoit, Pierre	*The Passion and Resurrection of Jesus Christ*	1969	O.P., Lectorate in theology	Priest	Catholic
52 (48)	Benson, George	*A Summary View of the Evidences of Christ's Resurrection*	1754	D.D.	Minister	Presbyterian
53 (49)	Benson, Richard Meux	*The Life Beyond the Grave*	1885	Christ Church	Priest	Anglican
54 (50)	Bernard, Pierre R.	*The Mystery of Jesus Vol. 2*	1996	O.P.	Priest	Catholic
55 (51)	Bevan, William	*The Coming of Christ*	1889	Huron College	Reverend	Anglican
56 (52)	Bewes, Richard	*The Resurrection: Fact or Fiction?*	1989	O.B.E. and M.A.	Minister	Anglican
57 (53)	Bible, Andrew F.	*Jesus and the Resurrection*	1890	—	English	—
58 (54)	Bieringer, Reimund, and Jan Lambrecht	*Resurrection in the New Testament*	2002	Defended his doctorate	Professor of New Testament exegesis	Catholic

59 (55)	Bigland, John	*Reflections on the Resurrection and Ascension of Christ*	1803	No formal education	School master	—
60 (56)	Binz, Stephen J.	*The Resurrection & The Life*	2006	Graduate studies	Biblical scholar	Catholic
61 (56)		*The Passion and Resurrection Narratives of Jesus*	1989			
62 (57)	Biser, Eugen	*The Light of the Lamb*	1961	D.Th. and D.Phil.	Priest	Catholic
63 (58)	Bishop, Hugh	*The Easter Drama*	1958	C.R.	Member of C.R.	Catholic
64 (59)	Bligh, John	*The Sign of the Cross: The Passion and Resurrection of Jesus*	1975	S.J.	Priest	Catholic
65 (60)	Blomberg, Craig L. and Carl Stecher	*Faith or Fact?*	2019	Ph.D	New Testament scholar	—
66 (61)	Blunt, John J.	*Principles for the Proper Understanding of the Mosaic Writings*	1833	St. John's College	Priest	Anglican

67 (62)	Boardman, George Dan	*Our Risen King's Forty Days*	1902	Newton Theological Institution	Clergymen	Baptist
68 (62)		*Epiphanies of the Risen Lord*	1879			
69 (63)	Bode, Edward Lynn	*The First Easter Morning*	1970	Degrees in Sacred Scripture	Priest	Catholic
70 (64)	Body, George	*The Appearances of the Risen Lord: Practical Readings*	1889	Honorary D.D.	D.D.	Anglican
71 (65)	Boff, Leonardo	*The Question of Faith in the Resurrection of Jesus*	1971	Studied theology	Professor of theology	Catholic
72 (66)	Boice, James	*The Christ of the Empty Tomb*	1985	Honorary D.D.	Reformed theologian	Presbyterian
73 (67)	Bold, Thomas Arthur	*New Testament Evidence for the Resurrection*	1925	M.A.	Reverend	—
74 (68)	Bombaro, John J., and Adam S. Francisco	*The Resurrection Fact*	2016	Ph.D.	Missionary	Lutheran

75 (69)	Bonnke, Reinhard	*Explosion of Life: The World Drama of Resurrection*	1994	Bible College of Wales	Evangelist	Pentecostal
76 (70)	Borg, Marcus J., and John Dominic Crossan	*The Last Week*	2007	Ph.D.	Theologian	Episcopalian
77 (71)	Bornhäuser, Karl	*The Death and Resurrection of Jesus Christ*	1958	Studied theology	New Testament theologian	Lutheran
78 (72)	Bounds, Edward McKendree	*The Ineffable Glory: Thoughts on the Resurrection*	1921	Layperson	Author	Methodist
79 (72)	Bounds, Edward McKendree	*The Resurrection*	1907	Layperson	Author	Methodist
80 (73)	Bourgy, Paul	*The Resurrection of Christ and of Christians*	1963	O.P.	Theologian.	Catholic
81 (74)	Bowen, Clayton Raymond	*The Resurrection in the New Testament*	1911	B.D., M.Div., and Th.D.	Pastor	Unitarian
82 (75)	Bowman, Robert M.	*Jesus' Resurrection and Joseph's Visions*	2020	Ph.D.	President	Christian

83 (76)	Brookes, James H.	*Did Jesus Rise? A Book Written to Aid Honest Skeptics*	1945	Honorary D.D.	Minister	Presbyterian
84 (76)		*He is Not Here: The Resurrection of Christ*	1896			
85 (77)	Brookhart, C. Franklin	*Living the Resurrection: Reflections After Easter*	2012	M.Div. and D.Min.	Bishop	Episcopalian
86 (78)	Broughton, William P.	*The Historical Development of Legal Apologetics*	2009	M.Div. and D.Min.	Pastor	Christian
87 (79)	Brown, James Baldwin	*The Risen Christ, the King of Men*	1890	B.A.	Minister	Non-conformist
88 (80)	Brown, Michael	*Resurrection*	2020	Ph.D.	Radio host	Messianic Jewish
89 (81)	Brown, Raymond E.	*A Risen Christ in Eastertime*	1991	Ph.D.	Priest	Catholic
90 (81)		*The Virginal Conception and Bodily Resurrection*	1973			

91 (82)	Bruce, David	*The Resurrection of History*	2014	Ph.D.	Associate Executive Director	Catholic
92 (83)	Brumback, Carl	*Accent on the Ascension!*	1955	Central Bible Institute	Minister	Protestant
93 (84)	Brundrit, Daniel Femley	*Is the Resurrection True?*	1934	Layperson	Barrister-at-law	—
94 (85)	Bryan, Christopher	*The Resurrection of the Messiah*	2011	Ph.D.	Priest	Anglican
95 (86)	Bryan, David K., and David W. Pao	*Ascent into Heaven in Luke-Acts*	2016	Ph.D.	Director of TEDS	Presbyterian
96 (87)	Bryan, Lyman	*The Easter Story: The Story of Jesus*	1941		—	
97 (88)	Bryant, Robert A.	*The Risen Crucified Christ in Galatia*	2001	Ph.D.	Professor	Presbyterian
98 (89)	Buck, Daniel Dana	*Our Lord's Great Prophecy*	1856	Honorary D.D.	Preacher	Methodist

99 (90)	Budd, Leonard H. and Roger G. Talbott	*Resurrection Promises*	1987	M.A. and D.Min.	Minister	Methodist
100 (91)	Bürgener, Karsten	*The Resurrection of Christ from the Dead*	1978	Studied theology	Priest	Lutheran
101 (92)	Burgess, Andrew R.	*The Ascension in Karl Barth*	2004	M.Th. and D. Phil.	Deacon	Anglican
102 (93)	Burrell, David James	*The Resurrection and the Life Beyond*	1920	—	Theologian	Presbyterian
103 (94)	Bush, George	*The Resurrection of Christ in Answer to the Question Whether He Rose*	1845	College graduate	Biblical scholar	Presbyterian
104 (95)	Busse, Roger S.	*Jesus, Resurrected: Risk Analysis and Recovery*	2017	Reed College and Harvard Divinity School	CEO	Christian
105 (96)	Butcher, John Beverley	*Telling the Untold Stories: Encounters with the Resurrected Jesus*	2000	M.Div.	Priest	United Church of Christ
106 (97)	Butler, Samuel	*The Evidence for the Resurrection*	1865	St. John's College	Novelist	—

107 (98)	Buttrick, David G.	*The Mystery and the Passion*	1992	B.D.	Minister	Presbyterian
108 (99)	Calhoun, John M.	*The Resurrection of the Post Resurrection Appearances of Jesus Christ*	2021	D.D.	Writer	Baptist
109 (100)	Candler, Warren Akin	*Easter Meditations*	1930	Emory College	Bishop	Methodist
110 (101)	Cantalamessa, Raniero	*Easter: Meditations on the Resurrection*	2006	Ph.D.	Priest	Catholic
111 (102)	Capt. E. Raymond	*The Resurrection Tomb*	1988	Layman	General contractor	—
112 (103)	Carnley, Peter	*Resurrection in Retrospect PB*	2020	Trinity College, Emmanuel, and St. John's College	Archbishop of Perth	Anglican
113 (103)		*The Reconstruction of Resurrection Belief*	2019			
114 (103)		*The Structure of Resurrection Belief*	1987			

115 (104)	Carpenter, William Boyd	*Forty Days of the Risen Life*	1898	Liverpool Institute, St. Catherine's College	Cleric	Anglican
116 (105)	Carson, D. A.	*Scandalous: The Cross and Resurrection*	2010	Ph.D.	New Testament scholar	Baptist
117 (106)	Catchpole, David R.	*Resurrection People*	2000	PhD.	Professor of Theological Studies	—
118 (107)	Cattermole, Richard and Henry Stebbing	*Sacred Classics*	1835	B.D.	Cleric	Anglican
119 (108)	Cecilia, Madame Bowerman, Elizabeth	*From the Sepulchre to the Throne*	1914	Layperson	Congregation of Les Réligieuses de Saint-André	Catholic
120 (109)	Chaffey, Tim	*In Defense of Easter*	2014	Th.M., M.Div., and M.A.	Founder and director of Midwest Apologetics.	Christian
121 (110)	Chalakkal, Sebastian	*Resurrection Appearances in Contemporary Christology*	2009	Ph.D.	Priest	Catholic
122 (111)	Chandler, Samuel	*The Witnesses of the Resurrection*	1744	Samuel Jones Academy	Writer	Non-conformist

123 (112)	Chang, Rainbow	*Passion, Resurrection, and Ascension*	2020	Layperson	Fellow of the Royal Society of Arts	Anglican
124 (113)	Chapman, Raymond	*Stations of the Resurrection*	1998	Oxford and King's College	Priest	Anglican
125 (114)	Chappell, Wallace D.	*When Jesus Rose*	1972	Honorary doctorate	Pastor	Methodist
126 (115)	Charles, Elizabeth Rundle	*By Thy Glorious Resurrection and Ascension*	1888	Layperson	Writer	Anglican
127 (116)	Charlesworth, James H.	*Resurrection: The Origin and Future of a Biblical Doctrine*	2006	Ph.D.	Professor	Greek Orthodox
128 (117)	Chilton, Bruce S.	*Resurrection Logic*	2019	Ph. D.	Professor of Religion	Episcopalian
129 (118)	Chevrot, Georges	*On the Third Day: The Resurrection*	1961	—	Priest	Catholic
130 (119)	Chojnacki, Stanislaw	*Christ's Resurrection in Ethiopian Painting*	2009	M.A.	Professor	—

131 (120)	Chrispin, Gerad W.	*Were You There?*	2021	—	Criminal lawyer	—
132 (120)		*The Resurrection: The Unopened Gift*	1999			
133 (121)	Clark, Daniel	*Dead or Alive? The Truth and Relevance of Jesus' Resurrection*	2007	B.A.	Vicar	Anglican
134 (122)	Clark, Neville	*Interpreting the Resurrection. 2nd ed.*	1967	M.A.	Scholar	Baptist
135 (123)	Cleveland, Rich	*The Words of the Risen Christ*	2007	B.S.	Founder of Emmaus Journey	Catholic
136 (124)	Clifford,	*Leading Lawyers Look at the Resurrection*	1991	B.Th. and Th.D.	Theologian	Baptist
137 (124)	Clifford, Ross, and Philip Johnson	*The Cross Is Not Enough*	2012	—		
138 (125)	Collins, John H.	*Risen as He Said*	1959	S.J.	Priest	Catholic

139 (126)	Collins, Thomas P.	*The Risen Christ in the Fathers of the Church*	1967	—	Instructor of theology	Catholic
140 (127)	Comblin, José	*The Resurrection in the Plan of Salvation*	1966	Ph.D.	Priest	Catholic
141 (128)	Conner, Walter Thomas	*The Resurrection of Jesus: A Message of Hope and Cheer*	1926	Ph.D	Theologian	Moderate Calvinist
142 (129)	Cook, George	*An Illustration of the General Evidence Establishing the Reality of Christ's Resurrection*	1826	D.D.	Minister	Presbyterian
143 (129)		*An Illustration of the General Evidence Establishing the Reality of Christ's Resurrection*	1808			
144 (130)	Cook, John Granger	*Empty Tomb, Resurrection, Apotheosis*	2018	Ph.D.	Professor of religion	—
145 (131)	Cooper, Thomas	*The Verity of Christ's Resurrection from the Dead*	1875	Layperson	Writer	—
146 (132)	Cox, Samuel	*The Resurrection: Twelve Expository Essays*	1881	D.D.	Pastor	Baptist

147 (133)	Craig, William Lane and Gerd Lüdemann	*Jesus' Resurrection: Fact or Figment?*	2000	Two Ph.Ds	Research professor of philosophy	Christian
148 (133)	Craig, William Lane, and John Dominic Crossan	*Will the Real Jesus Please Stand Up?*	1998	—	ǀ	ǀ
149 (133)	Craig, William Lane	*Assessing the New Testament Evidence*	1989	Ph.D.	Research professor	Christian
150 (133)		*Knowing the Truth about the Resurrection*	1988			
151 (133)		*The Historical Argument for the Resurrection*	1985			
152 (133)		*The Son Rises*	1981			
153 (134)	Cranfield, Thomas	*An Harmony of the Gospels*	1795	A.B.	ǀ	Anglican
154 (135)	Crawford, Dan R.	*Church Growth Words From the Risen Lord*	1990	M.Div. and D.Min.	Senior professor of Evangelism & Missions	Christian

155 (136)	Cromie, Richard M.	*Sometime Before the Dawn*	1982	D.D.	Pastor	Presbyterian
156 (137)	Croswell, Laurence	*It Is Finished: Passion, Death, and Resurrection*	2002	B.Ed.	Pastor	—
157 (138)	Crowder, Bill	*Windows on Easter*	2010	—	Pastor	—
158 (139)	Crowe, Bandon D.	*The Hope of Israel*	2020	Ph.D.	Professor of New Testament	Presbyterian
159 (140)	Culver, Robert Duncan, and Murray J. Harris	*A Wakeup Call*	1993	B.D., Th.M., and Th.D.	Professor of theology	Christian
160 (141)	Cummings, Brad	*Resurrection of the Divine*	2008	M.Div.	CEO of Windblown Media	Christian
161 (142)	Davies, John Gordon	*He Ascended into Heaven*	1958	Educated at King's School	Professor of theology	Anglican
162 (143)	Davis, Stephen T.	*Risen Indeed: Making Sense of the Resurrection*	1993	Ph.D.	Founder of Claremont McKenna College	Christian

163 (143)	Davis, Stephen T., et al.	*The Resurrection: An Interdisciplinary Symposium*	1997	—		
164 (144)	Dawe, Donald G.	*Jesus: The Death and Resurrection of God*	1985	Graduate study	Minister	Presbyterian
165 (145)	Dawson, Gerrit Scott	*Jesus Ascended*	2004	D.Min.	Minister	Presbyterian
166 (146)	Dawson, Ralph	*Was There a Resurrection?*	1977	Layperson	Film editor	—
167 (147)	Dawson, R. Dale	*The Resurrection in Karl Barth*	2007	M.Div. and D.Th.	Served in local church pastoral ministry	Protestant
168 (148)	Day, E. Hermitage	*On the Evidence for the Resurrection*	1906	D.D.	Vicar	Anglican
169 (149)	D' Costa, Gavin	*Resurrection Reconsidered*	1996	Ph.D.	Professor of theology	Catholic
170 (150)	Derrett, J. Duncan M.	*The Anastasis: The Resurrection of Jesus as an Historical Event*	1982	Ph.D.	Barrister	—

171 (151)	Dhanis, Édouard	*Resurrexit: Actes du Symposium International*	1974	—	Jesuit	Catholic
172 (152)	Dickinson, Richard William	*The Resurrection of Jesus Christ Historically and Logically Viewed*	1865	Yale	Minister	Presbyterian
173 (153)	Ditton, Humphry	*A Discourse Concerning the Resurrection of Jesus Christ*	1722	Studied theology	Mathematician	Non-conformist
174 (154)	Divine of the Church of England	*The History of the Incarnation, Life, Doctrine, and Miracles*	1737		—	
175 (155)	Doane, William Croswell	*The Book of Easter*	1910	University of PA	Bishop	Anglican
176 (155)		*The Manifestations of the Risen Jesus*	1898			

177 (156)	Dobson, Cyril Comyn	*The Risen Lord and His Disciples*	1935	M.A.	Vicar	Anglican
178 (156)		*The Empty Tomb and the Risen Lord*	1934			
179 (156)		*The Story of the Empty Tomb as If Told by Joseph of Arimathaea*	1920			
180 (157)	Dodson, Jonathan K., and Brad Watson.	*Raised? Finding Jesus by Doubting the Resurrection*	2014	M.Div. and Th.M.	Founding pastor of City Life Church	Christian
181 (158)	Donne, Brian K.	*Christ Ascended*	1983	M.A.	Minister	Baptist.
182 (159)	Dore, James	*An Essay on the Resurrection of Christ*	1797	A.M.	Pastor	Christian
183 (160)	Dowse, Edgar	*Christian Doctrine*	1986	Doctorate, six theology degrees	Priest	Anglican
184 (161)	Drinkwater, Francis Harold	*The Fact of the Resurrection*	1978	—	Priest	Catholic

185 (162)	Du Bose, Horace M.	*The Bodily Resurrection of Jesus Christ*	1924	Honorary D.D.	Bishop	Methodist
186 (163)	Dunn, James D.G.	*Why Believe in Jesus' Resurrection?*	2016	Ph.D. and D.D.	British New Testament scholar	Methodist
187 (164)	Durrwell, F.-X.	*Christ Our Passover*	2004	Theology degrees	Priest	Catholic
188 (165)		*The Resurrection: A Biblical Study*	1960			
189 (166)	Dyer, Keith D., and David J. Neville	*Resurrection and Responsibility*	2009	TPTC, B.A., B.Theol., and D.Theol.	Professor of New Testament	Baptist
190 (167)	Dymski, J. Daniel	*Stations of Joy*	2004	Completed seminary studies	Priest	Catholic
191 (168)	Eaton, Robert Ormston	*The Forty Days. Chapters on the Risen Life of our Lord*	1927	–	Priest	Catholic
192 (169)	Eckman, George P.	*When Christ Comes Again 2nd ed.*	1918	Ph.D.	Minister	Methodist

193 (170)	Edgar, R. McCheyne (of Dublin)	*The Gospel of a Risen Saviour*	1892	D.D.	Minister	Presbyterian
194 (170)		*The Resurrection of Jesus Christ*	1887			
195 (171)	Edmunds, Albert J.	*The Oldest Resurrection Documents*	1917	Layperson	Librarian	Society of Friends
196 (172)	Edwards, Mark Julian	*We Believe in the Crucified and Risen Lord*	2009	B.A., M.A., and D.Phil.	Tutor in theology	—
197 (173)	Elliott, Edward King	*From Death to Res urrection*	1907	A.M. and M.A.	Deacon	Anglican
198 (174)	Ellis, Eric Kent	*The Power of His Resurrection*	1962	—	Vicar	—
199 (175)	Elson, Edward L. R.	*And Still He Speaks: The Words of the Living Christ*	1960	D.D.	Minister	Presbyterian
200 (176)	Endsjo, Dag Øistein	*Greek Resurrection Beliefs and the Success of Christianity*	2009	Ph.D.	Professor of Religious Studies	—

201 (177)	Evans, Christopher Francis	*Resurrection and the New Testament*	1970	Corpus Christ College	Deacon	Anglican
202 (178)	Evans, Craig A.	*Jesus, the Final Days*	2009	Ph.D.	Professor of New Testament	Christian
203 (179)	Evans, William	*From the Upper Room to the Empty Tomb*	1934	D.D.	Theologian	Presbyterian
204 (180)	Évely, Louis	*Joy*	1968	Degrees in law and philosophy	Priest	Catholic
205 (181)	Ewen, Pamela Binnings	*Faith on Trial*	1999	Layperson	Lawyer	Christian
206 (182)	Farrow, Douglas	*Ascension and Ecclesia*	1999	B.R.E., M. Div., Th.M., and D. Phil.	Professor of theology	Catholic
207 (183)	Faunce, Daniel Worcester	*Advent and Ascension*	1903	D.D.	Minister	Baptist
208 (184)	Fenton, John. C.	*Preaching the Cross*	1958	D.D.	Deacon	Anglican

209 (185)	Fernando, Mark	*Questions You Always Wanted to Ask about Easter*	2005	—	Bible teacher	—
210 (186)	Filson, Floyd V.	*Jesus Christ, the Risen Lord*	1956	Th.D.	Minister	Presbyterian
211 (187)	Fishel, Kent M.	*Resurrection Evidences: A Bible Study.*	1985	Taylor University	Evangelist	Christian
212 (188)	Flood, Edmund	*The Resurrection*	1973	—	Benedictine monk	Catholic
213 (189)	Flynn, Leslie B.	*Day of Resurrection*	1965	D.D.	Minister	Baptist
214 (190)	Ford, D. W. Cleverley	*Preaching the Risen Christ*	1988	London College of Divinity	Archbishop of Canterbury	Anglican
215 (191)	Ford-Grabowsky, Mary	*Stations of the Light*	2005	Ph.D.	Professor in religious studies	—
216 (192)	Foster, Charles A.	*The Jesus Inquest*	2010	Ph.D.	Writer	—

217 (193)	Fraser, Neil McCormick	*The Glory of His Rising*	1963	—	Involved in ministry work	—
218 (194)	Fredrick, William	*Infallible Proof by Three Immutable Witnesses*	1916	—	Lived in Clyde, Ohio	—
219 (195)	Frick, Philip Louis	*The Resurrection and Paul's Argument*	1912	D.D.	Pastor	Methodist
220 (196)	Frye, Edwin Gibson	*Breakfast with the Risen Lord*	1938	Two honorary D.D.s	Pastor	Brethren Church
221 (197)	Fudge, Edward William	*Resurrection! Essays in Honor of Homer Hailey.*	1973	M.A.	Theologian	Christian
222 (198)	Fuller, Daniel Payton	*Easter Faith and History*	1965	B.D., Th.M., Th.D., and D. Th.	Professor of hermeneutics	Protestant
223 (199)	Fuller, Reginald H.	*The Formation of the Resurrection Narratives*	1971	M.A. and S.T.D.	Priest	Episcopalian
224 (200)	Fullmer, Paul M.	*Resurrection in Mark's Literary-Historical Perspective*	2007	Ph.D.	Ordination	Presbyterian

225 (201)	Furness, William Henry	*The Story of the Resurrection of Christ Told Once More*	1885	D.D.	Clergyman	Unitarian
226 (202)	Gaddy, C. Welton	*Easter Proclamation: Remembrance, and Renewal*	1974	Ph.D.	President Emeritus of Interfaith Alliance	Baptist
227 (203)	Gansky, Alton	*40 Days: Encountering Jesus between the Resurrection and Ascension.*	2007	Honorary D.D.	Novelist	—
228 (204)	Gant, Peter R.	*Seeing Light: An Enquiry into the Origins of Resurrection Faith*	2019	B.D.	Parish vicar	Anglican
229 (205)	Garbutt, Richard	*Demonstration of the Resurrection*	1657 (1669 reprint)	B.A., B.D., and M.A.	Cambridge	Puritan
230 (206)	Gardner-Smith, Percival	*The Narratives of the Resurrection*	1926	B.D. and M.A.	Deacon	Anglican
231 (207)	Garrott, John	*The Unseen Presence: Encounters on the Emmaus Road*	2003	B.A. and M.Div.	Reverend	Methodist
232 (208)	Gault, Clarence W.	*Indebted to Christ's Resurrections*	1956	Th.M.	Minister	Presbyterian

233 (209)	Geering, Lloyd George	*Resurrection: A Symbol of Hope*	1971	Honorary D.D.	Professor of Religious Studies	Presbyterian
234 (210)	Geis, Robert J.	*The Christ from Death Arisen*	2008	Pursued graduate scripture courses in Hebrew	Prelate Protosyncellus	Orthodox
235 (211)	Geisler, Norman L.	*The Battle for the Resurrection*	2004	Ph.D.	Systematic theologian	Evangelical Christian
236 (211)		*In Defense of the Resurrection*	1991			
237 (211)		*The Battle for the Resurrection*	1989			
238 (212)	Gibbins, Ronald C.	*The Stations of the Resurrection*	1988	Didsbury College	Minister	Methodist
239 (213)	Gilchrist, James Michael	*Jesus! What Was That?*	2007	Ph.D.	Humanist	—
240 (214)	Goergen, Donald J.	*The Death and Resurrection of Jesus*	1988	Ph.D.	Friar	Catholic

241 (215)	Goldstein, Clifford	*Risen: Finding Hope in the Empty Tomb*	2020	M.A.	Leading figure in the Seventh-day Adventist movement	Secular Jew
242 (216)	Gooder, Paula	*Journey to the Empty Tomb*	2015	D.Phil.	Lecturer	Anglican
243 (216)		*This Risen Existence*	2015			
244 (217)	Goodier, Alban	*The Risen Jesus: Meditations*	1948	B.A. and later S.J.	Priest	Catholic
245 (218)	Goodwin, Thomas	*Christ Set Forth, in His Death, Resurrection, Ascension*	1846 [Original 1651]	B.A.	Theologian	Congregational
246 (218)		*The Glories of Christ Set Forth*	1817			
247 (219)	Goppelt, Leonhard	*The Easter Message Today: Three Essays*	1964	Ph.D.	New Testament exegete	Protestant

248 (220)	Green, Michael	*The Empty Cross of Jesus*	1984	Honorary D.D.	Evangelist	Anglican
249 (220)		*The Day Death Died*	1982			
250 (220)		*Man Alive!*	1968			
251 (221)	Greenhalgh, John	*If Christ Be Not Risen . . .'*	1986	—		
251 (222)	Grey, Mary C.	*The Resurrection of Peace*	2012	Ph.D.	Theologian	Catholic
252 (223)	Grierson, Herbert John Clifford	*And the Third Day... : A Record of Hope and Fulfilment*	1948	LL.D., Litt. D., F.B.A.	Literary scholar	—
253 (224)	Grierson, James	*Scenes and Interviews with the Risen Saviour*	1869	D.D.	Minister	Presbyterian
254 (224)		*Heaven on Earth*	1856			

255 (225)	Grieve, Val	*Your Verdict on the Empty Tomb*	1996	Law graduate	Solicitor	Christian
256 (226)	Griffin, James Anthony, Bishop	*Easter Joy*	2007	Pontifical Lateran University	Prelate of the Roman Catholic Church	Catholic
257 (227)	Grove, Henry	*The Evidence for Our Saviour's Resurrection Consider'd*	1730	Taunton Dissenting Academy.	Minister	Non-conformist
258 (228)	Guinness, Howard	*Call the Witnesses: St. Paul on Trial*	1969	Layperson	United Kingdom Rector	Anglican
259 (229)	Gunter, W. Stephen	*Resurrection Knowledge: Recovering the Gospel*	1999	Ph.D.	Professor Emeritus of Evangelism	Methodist
260 (230)	Gurney, Thomas Alfred	*Alive for Evermore*	1930	B.A., M.A., and LL.B.	Deacon	Anglican

				Ph.D.	Theologian	Evangelical
261 (231)	Habermas, Gary R.	*On the Resurrection,* (Volume 1: Evidences)	2024 forthcoming			
261 (231)		*Risen Indeed: A Historical Investigation*	2021			
262 (231)		*The Resurrection of Jesus Handbook*	2014			
263 (231)		*Did the Resurrection Happen?*	2009			
264 (231)		*Resurrected? An Atheist and Theist Dialogue*	2005			
265 (231)		*The Case for the Resurrection of Jesus*	2004			
266 (231)		*The Risen Jesus & Future Hope*	2003			
267 (231)		*The Resurrection: Heart of the New Testament. Vol. 1.*	2000			

268 (231)		*The Resurrection: Heart of the New Testament. Vol. 2.*	2000			
269 (231)		*Did Jesus Rise from the Dead? The Resurrection Debate*	1987			
270 (231)		*The Resurrection of Jesus: An Apologetic*	1980			
271 (232)	Hailey, O. L.	*The Three Prophetic Days of Matt. 12:40*	1931	D.D.	Pastor	Baptist
272 (233)	Hales, Bruce David	*Walking in Newness of Life*	2012	Layperson	Businessman	Brethren Christian Church
273 (234)	Hall, Alvin. Willard	*Resurrection of Christ and What It Stands For*	1905	General Theological Seminary and Western Theological Seminary	Reverend	Methodist
274 (235)	Hall, Francis J.	*The Passion and Exaltation of Christ*	1918	D.D.	Deacon	Episcopalian
275 (236)	Hall, Jean	*Out of Easter, the Gospels*	1979	Layperson	—	—

276 (237)	Hallett, Joseph II	*Christ's Ascension into Heaven Asserted*	1693	Educated by his father	Minister	Non-conformist
277 (238)	Han, Cheon-Seol	*Raised for Our Justification*	1995	Ph.D.	South Korean	—
278 (239)	Hanegraaff, Hank	*The Third Day: The Reality of the Resurrection*	2003	No formal education	Author	Greek Orthodox
279 (239)		*Resurrection*	2000			
280 (240)	Hanna, William	*The Forty Days After Our Lord's Resurrection*	1863	Honorary D.D.	Minister	Presbyterian
281 (241)	Hanson, George	*The Resurrection and the Life*	1912	D.D.	Reverend	Presbyterian
282 (242)	Hanson, Richard Simon	*Journey to Resurrection*	1986	Ph.D.	Chaplain	Christian
283 (243)	Harden, Ralph William	*The Evangelists and the Resurrection*	1914	B.A.	Rector	Anglican

284 (244)	Hare, Augustus William	*Letters to the Editor of The New Trial of the Witnesses*	1824	A.M.	Writer	Anglican
285 (245)	Harries, Richard	*Christ Is Risen*	1988	B.A. and M.A.	Bishop of Oxford	Anglican
286 (246)	Harris, Greg (Gregory H.)	*The Darkness and the Glory*	2008	M.Div., Th.M., and Th.D.	Pastor	Christian
287 (247)	Harris, Murray J.	*From Grave to Glory: Resurrection in the New Testament*	1990	Ph.D.	Warden of Tyndale House	Christian Brethren Assembly
288 (247)		*Raised Immortal*	1985			
289 (248)	Hartill, Isaac	*The Ascension of Our Lord Jesus Christ*	1902	Honorary D.D.	Reverend	Congregational
290 (249)	Harvey, L. James	*The Resurrection: Ruse or Reality?*	2011	Ph.D.	High school coach	Christian
291 (250)	Harvey, Nicholas Peter	*Death's Gift*	1995	—	Tutor	Catholic

292 (251)	Hastings, W. Ross	*The Resurrection of Jesus Christ*	2022	M.A. and Ph.Ds.	Professor of Theology	—
293 (252)	Hayes, Doremus A.	*The Resurrection Fact*	1932	Ph.D.	Preacher	Methodist
294 (253)	Hays, Steve	*This Joyful Eastertide*	2006	B.A.	Calvinist	Christian
295 (254)	Head, Edward Douglas	*Burning Hearts*	1947	M.Th. and D.Th.	President of Southwestern Baptist Theological Seminary	Baptist
296 (255)	Head, Peter M.	*Proclaiming the Resurrection*	1998	Ph.D.	Member of the Faculty of Theology and Religion	—
297 (256)	Heath, Dale E.	*The Risen-Christ Scriptures*	1994	Ph.D.	Professor	Methodist
298 (257)	Hendrickx, Herman	*The Resurrection Narratives of the Synoptic Gospels*	1984	B.A. and Licentiate in theology	Professor of New Testament studies	Catholic
299 (258)	Heuschen, Joseph Maria	*The Bible on the Ascension*	1965	Ph.D.	Professor	Catholic

300 (259)	Hewson, John	*Christ Rejected*	1832	—	Pastor	Christian
301 (260)	Hickling, Stewart Ross	*An Evidentiary Analysis of Doctor Richard Carrier's Objections to the Resurrection*	2018	Ph.D.	Founder of Shield Your Faith Ministry	Christian
302 (261)	Hill, William Bancroft	*The Resurrection of Jesus Christ: A New Study*	1930	Harvard University and Union Theological Seminary	Minister	Reformed Church
303 (262)	Hindmarsh, Robert	*An Essay on the Resurrection of the Lord*	1833–77	No formal education	Printer	Swedenborgian
304 (263)	Hoadley, Burton James	*Two Morning.*	1925	—	Reverend	Christian
305 (264)	Hoare, Rodney	*Testimony of the Shroud*	1978	M.A.	Chairman of the British Society for The Turin Shroud	Anglican
306 (265)	Hobbs, Herschel H.	*Messages on the Resurrection*	1959	Ph.D. and D.D.	President of the Southern Baptist Convention	Baptist
307 (266)	Holding, James Patrick	*Defending the Resurrection*	2010	M.A.	Founder of Tekton Education and Apologetic Ministries	Christian

308 (267)	Hollis, Gertrude	*But Chiefly A Help to Easter Gladness*	1920	Layperson	Author	—
309 (268)	Holloway, David	*Where did Jesus Go?*	1983	—	Parish minister	Episcopalian
310 (269)	Holzapfel, Richard Neitzel	*A Lively Hope: The Suffering, Death, Resurrection, and Exaltation*	1999	Ph.D.	Professor of Church History and Doctrine	Church of Latter-day Saints
311 (270)	Hooke, Samuel Henry	*The Resurrection of Christ as History and Experience*	1967	Ph.D.	Professor of Oriental Languages	Anglican
312 (271)	Hoskyns, Edwyn Clement	*Crucifixion— Resurrectio:*	1981	D.D.	Priest	Anglican
313 (272)	Houlden, J. Leslie	*Backward into Light*	1987	Queen's College	Deacon, priest, and academic.	Anglican
314 (273)	Houselander, Caryll	*The Risen Christ: The Forty Days after the Resurrection*	1958	Layperson	Ecclesiastical artist	Catholic
315 (274)	Howe, Fisher	*The True Site of Calvary*	1871	Layperson	Merchant	Presbyterian

316 (275)	Hugh, Bishop	*The Easter Drama*	1958	C.R.	Bishop	Catholic
317 (276)	Huntington, F.D.	*A Harmony of the Gospel Narratives*	1889	D.D.	Clergyman	Episcopalian
318 (277)	Hutson, Curtis	*Great Preaching on the Resurrection*	1984	Layperson	Pastor	Baptist
319 (278)	Ide, Arthur Frederick	*The Resurrection: An Analysis*	1999	D.Phil.	Author	—
320 (278(		*Resurrection, Sex, and God*	1990			
321 (269)	Ingram, Joseph Edward	*On the Witness Stand, He Who Was and Now Is.*	1931	Layperson	Lawyer	—
322 (270)	Ireson, Gordon Worley	*Victory: The Gospel of The Resurrection*	1970	—	Canon of Newcastle	Anglican
323 (271)	Jacob, Jim	*A Lawyer's Case for the Resurrection*	2016	—	Attorney	Christian

324 (272)	Jacob, of Serug	Jacob of Sarug's Homilies	—	—	Bishop	Catholic
325 (273)	Jacobovici, Simcha	The Jesus Family Tomb	2007	M.A.	Film director	—
326 (274)	Jaki, Stanley L.	Resurrection	2004	Ph.D.	Priest	Catholic
327 (275)	Jansen, John Frederick	The Resurrection of Jesus Christ in New Testament Theology	1980	Th.D.	Pastor	Presbyterian
328 (275)		No Idle Tale	1967			
329 (276)	Jennings, Abraham Gould.	The Last Days of Jesus Christ	1893	Layperson	Businessman	Presbyterian
329 (277)	Jensen, Matthew D.	Affirming the Resurrection of the Incarnate Christ	2012	Ph.D.	Teaching New Testament	—
330 (278)	Jeremiah, David	Christ's Death & Resurrection	1997	Honorary D.D.	Pastor	Christian

331 (279)	John Paul II, Pope	*Rising in Christ*	2004	Two Doctorates and a Licentiate of Sacred Theology	Bishop of Rome, head of the Roman Catholic Church	Catholic
332 (280)	John-Charles, Peter	*When Was Christ's Death and Resurrection?*	2001	Ph.D.	Works in computing	—
333 (281)	Johnson, Clifford Ross	*Every Moment: An Easter*	1962	B.D., M.A., and Doctorate	Pastor	Presbyterian
334 (282)	Johnson, Jeremiah J.	*Body of Proof: the 7 Best Reasons to Believe in the Resurrection*	2023	Ph.D.	New Testament scholar	Christian
335 (283)	Johnson, Kim Allan	*The Morning: His Empty Tomb Means More than You Ever Dreamed*	2002	M.Div.	Pastor	Seventh-day Adventist
336 (284)	Johnson, Luke Timothy	*Living Jesus*	1998	Ph.D.	Professor of New Testament and Christian Origins	Catholic
337 (285)	Judson, Albert	*Scripture Questions Concerning the Life, Death Resurrection and Ascension*	1825	Yale College	Pastor	Presbyterian
338 (286)	Kadlecek, Jo	*A Desperate Faith: Lessons of Hope*	2010	Layperson	Journalist	—

339 (287)	Kankaanniemi, Matti	*The Guards of the Tomb: Matthew's Apologetic Legend Revisited*	2010	Ph.D.	Pastor	ǀ
340 (288)	Kartsonis, Anna D.	*Anastasis: The Making of an Image*	1986	Ph.D.	Professor emeritus	ǀ
341 (289)	Kee, Alistair	*From Bad Faith to Good News: Reflections*	1991	College graduate	Head of the department of Religious Studies	ǀ
342 (290)	Keigwin, John	*Mount Calvary, or, The History of the Passion, Death, and Resurrection*	1826	Layperson	Antiquarian	ǀ
343 (291)	Keller, Timothy	*Hope in Times of Fear*	2020	M.Div. and D.Min.	Ordained by the Presbyterian Church in America	Presbyterian
344 (292)	Kelly, Anthony	*Upward: Faith, Church, and the Ascension*	2014	CSsR., STL., D. Theol., and F.A.C.T.A.	Priest	Catholic
345 (292)		*The Resurrection Effect*	2008			

346 (293)	Kelsey, Morton T.	*The Drama of the Resurrection*	1999	Episcopal Theological School	Priest	Episcopalian
346 (293)		*Resurrection, Release from Oppression*	1985			
347 (294)	Kena, Kwasi Issa	*The Resurrected Jesus*	2001	Layperson	College professor	Methodist
348 (295)	Kennedy, D. James	*Who Is This Jesus, Is He Risen?*	2002	Ph.D.	Pastor	Presbyterian
349 (296)	Kennedy, John	*The Resurrection of Jesus Christ: An Historical Fact*	1871	D.D.	Minister	Congregational
350 (297)	Kepler, Thomas S.	*The Meaning and Mystery of the Resurrection*	1963	Cornell University, Boston University School of Theology	Professor of New Testament	Methodist
351 (298)	Kerr, Hugh Thomson	*After He Had Risen*	1934	Western Theological Seminary	Chaplain	Presbyterian
352 (299)	Kesich, Veselin	*The First Day of the New Creation*	1982	Ph.D.	Professor emeritus of New Testament	Orthodox Church

351 (300)	Kessler, William Thomas	*Peter as the First Witness of the Risen Lord*	1998	Ph.D.	Priest	Catholic
352 (301)	King, Geoffrey R.	*The Forty Days*	1962	—	Pastor	Baptist
353 (302)	Kirkland, Winifred	*The Continuing Easter*	1943	Layperson	Private school teacher	—
354 (303)	Kirkpatrick, Kathy Newell	*He Is Risen! He Is Risen Indeed!*	1994	Layperson	Reverend	—
355 (304)	Klopstock, Friedrich Gottlieb	*The Messiah*	1817	Layperson	Poet	—
356 (305)	Knowles, Archibald Campbell	*The Triumph of the Cross: A Devotional Study*	1900	D.D.	Deacon	Anglican
357 (306)	Knowles, Michael P.	*The Third Voice*	2021	M.Div. and D.Th.	Ordained in the Church of Canada	Anglican
358 (307)	Koester, Craig R.	*The Resurrection of Jesus in the Gospel of John*	2008	Ph.D.	Parish pastor	Lutheran

359 (308)	Krummacher, Friedrich W.	*The Risen Redeemer*	1863	Studied theology	Theologian	Protestant
360 (309)	Künneth, Walter	*The Theology of the Resurrection*	1965	D.Phil.	Theologian	Protestant
361 (310)	Kuyper, Abraham	*The Death and Resurrection of Christ*	1888 [1960 trans]	D.Th.	Theologian	Protestant
362 (311)	Ladd, George Eldon	*I Believe in the Resurrection of Jesus*	1975	Ph.D.	Minister	Baptist
363 (312)	Lake, Kirsopp	*The Historical Evidence for the Resurrection*	1907	Cuddesdon Theological College	Priest	Anglican
364 (313)	Lampe, G. W. H. and Donald MacKinnon.	*The Resurrection: A Dialogue*	1966	Exeter College	Priest	Anglican
365 (314)	Landels, William	*The Sepulchre in the Garden*	1867	D.D.	Minister	Baptist
366 (315)	Lange, Reinhold	*The Resurrection*	1967	Layperson	Art historian	—

367 (316)	Lapide, Pinchas	*The Resurrection: A Jewish Perspective*[32]	1983	—	Historian	Jewish
368 (317)	La Potterie, Ignace de.	*The Hour of Jesus*	1989	Ph.D.	Priest	Catholic
369 (318)	Latham, Henry	*The Risen Master: A Sequel to Pastor Pastorum*	1901	D.D.	Deacon	Anglican
370 (319)	Laurie, Greg	*Why the Resurrection? A Personal Guide*	2004	No formal seminary degree	Graphic designer and pastor	Christian
371 (320)	Lavoie, Gilbert R	*Resurrected: Tangible Evidence That Jesus Rose from the Dead*	2000	M.D.	Medical doctor	—
372 (321)	Layton, Bentley	*The Gnostic Treatise on Resurrection from Nag Hammadi*	1979	Ph.D.	Professor emeritus of Religious	—
373 (322)	Lee, Robert Greene	*A Grand-Canyon of Resurrection Realities*	1935	Furman University	Pastor	Baptist

---

[32] Richardsh, a Messianic Jewish teacher in the UK, in a blog post says, "His book "*The Resurrection of Jesus*" takes liberal theologians to task for denying the resurrection of Jesus, but his own views are not always clear, and capable of various interpretations."

374 (323)	Leeper, Wayne D.	*Prelude to Glory: Insights into the Death, Burial and Resurrection*	1987	—	Accountant	Christian
375 (324)	Léon-Dufour, Xavier	*Resurrection and the Message of Easter*	1975	S.J.	Priest	Catholic
376 (325)	Lewis, Alan E.	*Cross and Resurrection: A Theology*	2001	—	Professor of constructive and modern theology	Presbyterian
377 (326)	Licona, Michael R.	*The Resurrection of Jesus: A New Historiographical Approach*	2010	Ph.D.	Associate professor in theology	Christian
378 (326)		*Paul Meets Muhammad*	2006			
379 (327)	Liddon, H. P.	*Easter in St. Paul's*	1877	King's College, Christ Church	Theologian	Anglican
380 (328)	Lilley, James Samuel	*Was the Resurrection a Fact?*	1916	—	Pastor	Methodist
381 (329)	Linton, Henry	*Jesus and the Resurrection*	1865	M.A.	Fellow of Magdalen College	Anglican

382 (330)	Lipscomb, A. A.	*Studies in the Forty Days*	1884	No formal education	Clergyman	Methodist
383 (331)	Little, Sophia L.	*The Birth, Last Days, and Resurrection of Jesus*	1841	Layperson	Poet	—
384 (332)	Loane, Marcus L.	*Jesus Himself: The Story of the Resurrection*	2007	Moore Theological College	Bishop	Anglican
385 (332)		*Our Risen Lord*	1968			
386 (332)		*Then Came Jesus*	1967			
386 (332)		*It Is The Lord*	1965			
387 (332)		*The Prince of Life*	1947			
388 (333)	Lockton, William	*The Resurrection and Other Gospel Narratives*	1924	B.D.	Vice-Principal	—

389 (334)	Loken, John	*The Shroud Was the Resurrection*	2006	M.A. and degrees in history and literature	—	Agnostic
390 (335)	Longenecker, Richard N.	*Life in the Face of Death*	1998	Ph.D.	New Testament scholar	Baptist
391 (336)	Lopez, René A.	*The Jesus Family Tomb Examined*	2008	Ph.D.	Assistant Professor of New Testament	Christian
392 (337)	Lorenzen, Thorwald	*Resurrection, Discipleship, Justice*	2003	Master's and doctorate in theology	Senior Minister	Baptist
393 (337)		*Resurrection and Discipleship*	1995			—
394 (338)	Lorimer, William	*Discourse of the Death and Resurrection of Christ*	1718	—	Minister	Reformed
395 (339)	Loughry, Joseph Nelson	*Christology*	1888	Princeton Theological Seminary	Pastor	Presbyterian
396 (340)	Lunn, Arnold	*The Third Day: A Defence of the Miracle of the Resurrection*	1945	Layperson	Catholic apologist	Catholic

397 (341)	Lunny, William J	*The Sociology of the Resurrection*	1989	—	Canadian deacon	Anglican
398 (342)	Luther, Martin	*The Martin Luther Easter Book*	1983 (repr.)	O.S.A. and D.Th.	Father of the Protestant Reformation.	Protestant
399 (343)	Macan, Reginald Walter	*Resurrection of Jesus Christ: An Essay in Three Chapters*	1877	D.Lit.	Fellow and Master at University College	Anglican
400 (344)	MacArthur, John	*The Resurrection of Jesus Christ*	1989	M.Div.	Pastor	Baptist
401 (345)	MacLaren, Alexander	*The Appearances of Our Lord After the Passion*	1912	Two honorary D.D.s	Minister	Baptist
402 (345)	Maclaren, Alexander, et al.	*The Empty Tomb: Resurrection Realities*	1896	—		
403 (345)	Maclaren, Alexander, et al.	*Great Sermons on the Resurrection*	1963	—		

404 (346)	MacMunn, Vivian Charles	*The Vision of the Young Man Menelaus*	1910	B.A.	Magistrate	Anglican
405 (346)		*Resurrectio Christi*	1909			
406 (347)	MacPherson, R. and D. Friedrich Strauss	*The Resurrection of Jesus Christ*	1867	D.D.	Professor of theology	Presbyterian
407 (348)	Mahoney, Robert	*Two Disciples at the Tomb*	1974	Ph.D.	Taught at the University of Saar	Catholic
408 (349)	Maloney, George A.	*The First Day of Eternity: Resurrection*	1982	Ph.D.	Priest	Eastern Orthodox
409 (350)	Marchant, James	*Theories of the Resurrection of Jesus Christ*	1899	FRSE, FLS FRAS KBE LLD.	Reverend	Presbyterian
410 (351)	Marsh, Frederick Edward	*The Resurrection of Christ: Fact or Fiction?*	1923	B.A. and F.R	Member of the Advent Testimony Movement	—
411 (351)		*What Does the Resurrection of Christ Mean?*	1901			

412 (352)	Martelet, Gustave	The Risen Christ and the Eucharistic World	1976	S.J.	Priest	Catholic
413 (353)	Martin, James D.	Did Jesus Rise from the Dead?	1956	Layperson	Professor of English	—
414 (354)	Martin, James Walter	A Critique on the Criticism on the Resurrection	1973	Southwestern Theological Seminary	Pastor	Baptist
415 (355)	Martin, Joseph	If the Tomb is Empty	2022	M. Div.	Founder and lead pastor of The Church of Eleven22	Christian
416 (356)	Marxsen, Willi	Jesus and Easter	1990	Ph.D.	Theologian	Protestant
417 (356)	Marxsen, Willi	The Resurrection of Jesus of Nazareth	1970	Ph.D.	Theologian	Protestant
418 (356)	Marxsen, Willi; and C. F. D. Moule	The Significance of the Message of the Resurrection	1968	—	—	—
419 (357)	Massee, Jasper Cortenus	After His Passion	1929	Mercer University	Pastor	Baptist

420 (358)	Massie, Edward	*The Risen Saviour*	1894	M.A.	Minister	—
421 (359)	Matera, Frank J.	*Resurrection: The Origin and Goal of the Christian Life*	2015	Ph.D.	Priest	Catholic
422 (360)	Mathewson, Steven D.	*Risen: 50 Reasons Why the Resurrection Changed Everything*	2013	Ph.D.	Pastor	Christian
423 (361)	McAllister, Dawson	*A Walk with Christ Through the Resurrection*	1981	Honorary D.D.	Author	Baptist
424 (362)	McCasland, S. Vernon	*The Resurrection of Jesus: A New Study*	1932	Ph.D.	Professor of religion	Disciples of Christ Church
425 (363)	McDonald, James Ian Hamilton	*The Resurrection: Narrative and Belief*	1989	Ph.D.	Reader	Christian
426 (364)	McDowell, Josh and Sean McDowell	*Resurrection and You*	2017	M.Div.	Evangelist	Christian

427 (364)	McDowell, Josh, and Dave Sterrett	*Did the Resurrection Happen— Really?*	2011	M.Div.	ǀ	
428 (364)		*Evidence for the Resurrection*	2009			
429 (364)		*Jesus: Dead or Alive? Teen Edition*	2009			
430 (364)	McDowell, Josh, et al.	*Jesus Is Alive! For Kids*	2009	M.Div.	ǀ	
431 (364)		*Resurrection Growth Guide*	1982			
432 (364)		*The Resurrection Factor*	1981			
433 (365)	McGarvey, J. W.	*Jesus and Jonah*	1896	College graduate	Minister	Protestant

434 (366)	McGee, J. Vernon	*The Empty Tomb: Proof of Life After Death*	1968	Ph.D.	Minister	Presbyterian
435 (366)		*After His Resurrection*	Nd.			
436 (367)	McGrath, Alister E.	*Resurrection*	2008	D.D.	Theologian	Anglican
437 (368)	McKay, Johnston R.	*Through Wood and Nails*	1983	Ph.D.	Assistant minister	Church of Scotland
438 (369)	McKenna, Megan	*And Morning Came: Scriptures of the Resurrection*	2003	Layperson	Theologian	Catholic
439 (370)	McKenzie, Leon	*Pagan Resurrection Myths and the Resurrection*	1997	Ph.D.	Priest	Catholic
440 (371)	McKenzie, Robert A.	*The First Day of the Week: The Mystery and Message*	1985	—	Reverend	Presbyterian
441 (372)	McKibbon, W. Stan	*The Anointed One*	1994	—	Founder of Stan McKibbon Ministries, Inc.	Christian

442 (373)	McKinley, J. L	*Jesus and the Resurrection*	2005	—	Summit Theological Seminary	—
443 (374)	McLeman, James	*Resurrection Then and Now*	1965 (repr. 1995)	—	Parish minister	—
444 (375)	Meadows, W. S. H.	*Alive from the Dead*	1869	M.A.	Reverend Rector	—
445 (376)	Merton, Thomas	*He Is Risen*	1975	M.A.	Trappist monk	Catholic
446 (377)	Michaelis, Johann David	*The Burial and Resurrection of Jesus Christ*	1827	Doctorate	Professor of theology	Protestant
447 (378)	Miller, Calvin	*The Christ of Easter*	2004	M.Div. and D.Min.	Pastor	Baptist
448 (379)	Miller, Laurence William	*Jesus Christ Is Alive*	1949	S.T.M. and S.T. D.	—	
449 (380)	Miller, Richard C.	*Resurrection and Reception in Early Christianity*	2015	Ph.D.	Adjunct professor	Renounced Christianity

450 (381)	Miller, Thomas A.	*Did Jesus Really Rise From the Dead?*	2013	M.D.	Professor of Surgery	—
451 (382)	Milligan, William	*The Ascension and Heavenly Priesthood of Our Lord*	1892	—		Presbyterian
452 (382)		*The Resurrection of Our Lord*	1881			
453 (383)	Mills, Watson E.	*Bibliographies on the Life and Teachings of Jesus. Vol. 8.*	2002	—	Minister	Christian
454 (384)	Minear, Paul S.	*To Die and to Live*	1977	Ph.D.	Professor Emeritus of Biblical Theology	Congregational
455 (385)	Mishkin, David	*Jewish Scholarship on the Resurrection of Jesus*	2017	Ph.D.	Serves on the faculty of Israel College of the Bible	Messianic Jew
456 (386)	M' Neile Hugh	*Lectures on the Sympathies, Sufferings, and Resurrection*	1843	D.D.	Evangelist	Anglican
457 (387)	Moberly, George	*The Sayings of the Great Forty Days*	1846	M.A.	Cleric	Anglican

458 (388)	Mohler, John Saylor	*The Resurrection*	1901	"Secured sufficient education to teach."	Bishop	United Brethren Church
459 (389)	Molnar, Paul D.	*Incarnation and Resurrection*	2007	Ph.D.	Professor of Systematic Theology	Catholic
460 (390)	Moloney, Francis J.	*The Resurrection of the Messiah*	2013	D.Phil., STL., and SSL.	Provincial Superior of the Salesians of Don Bosco	Catholic
461 (391)	Montefiore, Hugh	*Womb and the Tomb*	1992	B.D.	Bishop of Birmingham	Anglican
462 (392)	Moore, Thomas Vernor	*The Last Day of Jesus*	1858	D.D.	Pastor	Presbyterian
463 (393)	Morison, Frank [pseud. of Albert Henry Ross.]	*Who Moved the Stone*	1930	Layperson	Advertising agent	Christian
464 (394)	Morrison, Charles R.	*The Proofs of Christ's Resurrection*	1882	Studied law	Lawyer	Congregational
465 (395)	Mortimer, Alfred G.	*Jesus and the Resurrection; Thirty Addresses*	1898	D.D.	Rector	Episcopalian

466 (396)	Moss, Charles and William Bowyer	*The Evidence of the Resurrection Cleared*	1744	Norwich School and Caius College	Bishop of Bath and Wells	Anglican
467 (397)	Motter, Alton M.	*Preaching the Resurrection: Twenty-Two Great Easter Sermons*	1959	Gettysburg Theological Seminary	Pastor	Lutheran
468 (398)	Moule, C. F. D.	*Emmaus*	1912	Honorary D.D.	Priest	Anglican
469 (398)		*Jesus and the Resurrection: Expository Studies*	1893			
470 (399)	Mumaw, John R.	*The Resurrected Life*	1965	M.A.	Minister	Mennonite
471 (400)	Muncaster, Ralph	*What Is the Proof for the Resurrection?*	2000	B.S., and MBA.	Speaker	—
472 (401)	Murphy, Richard Thomas Aquinas	*Days of Glory*	1980	O.P., doctorates in Sacred Theology and Sacred Scripture	Taught at several parishes	Catholic
473 (402)	NeVille, Jeff	*His Final Days and Triumph*	2022	Doctor of Medical Dentistry	Dentist	Church of Latter-day Saints

474 (403)	Neyrey, Jerome H.	The Resurrection Stories	1988	Ph.D.	Priest	Catholic
475 (404)	Niebuhr, Richard R.	Resurrection and Historical Reason	1957	Ph.D.	Professor of divinity	Protestant
476 (405)	Noble, Samuel	The Rev. Samuel Noble on the Glorification of the Lord's Humanity	1856	—	Minister	Swedenborgian
477 (406)	Nott, Eliphalet	The Resurrection of Christ: A Series of Discourses	1872	Honorary D.D.	Minister	Presbyterian
478 (407)	Nouet, Jacques	The Life of Jesus Christ, in Glory on Earth	1846	S.J.	Priest	Catholic
479 (408)	Novakovic, Lidija	Resurrection: A Guide for the Perplexed	2016	Ph.D.	Professor of New Testament	—
480 (408)		Raised from the Dead According to Scripture	2012			
481 (409)	Nseka, Christian Kita	The Messiahship of the Lord	2009		—	

482 (410)	Ochsenford, Solomon Erb	*The Passion Story*	1889	D.D.	Pastor	Lutheran
483(411)	O' Collins, Gerald	*Saint Augustine on the Resurrection of Christ*	2017	S.J. and D.Th.	Priest	Catholic
484 (411)		*Believing in the Resurrection*	2012			
485 (411)		*Easter Faith: Believing in the Risen Jesus*	2003			
486 (411)		*The Resurrection of Jesus Christ*	1993			
487 (411)		*Interpreting the Resurrection*	1988			
488 (411)		*Jesus Risen*	1987			
489 (411)		*The Easter Jesus*	1980			

490 (411)		*What Are They Saying about the Resurrection?*	1978			
491 (411)		*The Resurrection of Jesus Christ*	1973			
492 (412)	O' Connell, Jake H.	*Jesus' Resurrection and Apparitions*	2016	—	Independent scholar	—
493 (413)	Olshausen, Hermann	*The Last Days of the Saviour*	1839	Universities	Theologian	Protestant
494 (414)	Olson, Carl E.	*Did Jesus Really Rise from the Dead?*	2016	M.Th.	Writer	Catholic
495 (415)	Ordal, Zacharias J.	*The Resurrection of Jesus: An Historical Fact*	1923	Luther Seminary	Minister	Lutheran
496 (416)	Orr, James	*The Resurrection of Jesus*	1908	D.D.	Minister	Presbyterian
497 (417)	Osborne, Grant R.	*The Resurrection Narratives: A Redactional Study*	1984	Ph.D.	Professor of New Testament	Evangelical

498 (418)	Pagán, Joshua A.	*Paul and the Resurrection*	2020	Ph.D.	Adjunct professor	Christian
499(419)	Palmer, Joseph	*The Central Event of Universal History*	1918	Private education	Stockbroker	Baptist
500 (420)	Parsons, Elmer E.	*Witness to the Resurrection*	1967	New York Biblical Seminary	Missionary	Methodist
501 (421)	Parsons, Mikeal C.	*The Departure of Jesus in Luke-Acts*	1987	Ph.D.	New Testament scholar	Baptist
502 (421)	Paternoster, Michael Cosgrove	*Stronger than Death*	1972	M.A.	Reverend Canon	Episcopalian
503 (422)	Paton, James	*The Glory and Joy of the Resurrection*	1902	D.D.	Missionary	Presbyterian
504 (423)	Patrick, Simon	*The Works of Symon Patrick. Vol. 3*	1858	B.D.	Theologian	Anglican
505 (423)		*Jesus and the Resurrection Justified*	1677 [1723]			

506 (424)	Pawson, David	*Explaining the Resurrection*	1993	M.Th.	Minister	Baptist
507 (425)	Paynter, Henry Martyn	*The Holy Resurrection: A Critical Exposition*	1884	A.M.	Minister	Presbyterian
508 (426)	Pearce, Zachary	*The Miracles of Jesus Vindicated*	1749	M.A.	Bishop of Bangor	Anglican
509 (427)	Perkins, Pheme	*Resurrection: New Testament Witness*	1984	Ph.D.	Professor of theology	Catholic
510 (428)	Perkins, Rufus Lord	*One Story: Four Parts*	1892	Layperson	Businessman	Presbyterian
511 (429)	Perrin, Norman	*The Resurrection According to Matthew, Mark, and Luke*	1977	M.Th. and D.Th.	Professor of New Testament	Christian
512 (430)	Perry, Charles Austin	*The Resurrection Promise*	1986	M.Div.	Provost	Episcopalian
513(431)	Perry, John M.	*Exploring the Resurrection of Jesus*	1993	Ph.D.	Professor of religious studies and philosophy	Catholic

514(432)	Perry, Michael C.	*The Easter Enigma*	1959	M.A.	Priest	Anglican
515 (433)	Peters, Ted, et. al.	*Resurrection: Theological and Scientific Assessments*	2002	Ph.D.	Minister	Lutheran
516 (434)	Peterson, Eugene H.	*Living The Resurrection*	2006	S.T.B.	Pastor	Presbyterian
517 (435)	Peterson, Paul K.	*Voices at the Crossroads*	1991	Drama degree	Pastor	Christian
518 (436)	Petty, Daniel W.	*Of First Importance: He Was Raised and Appeared*	2013	Ph.D.	Member of the American Society of Church History	Christian
519 (437)	Phillips, Forbes Alexander	*What Was the Resurrection?*	1910	Durham University	Chaplain	Anglican
520 (438)	Pine, Thomas	*Reflections on the Principles and Evidences of Christianity*	1835	—		Baptist
521 (439)	Pöelzl, Franz Xaver	*The Passion and Glory of Christ: A Commentary*	1919	Ph.D.	Professor of theology	Catholic

522 (440)	Pollard, George Frederick	*On the Third Day: Evidences for the Bodily Resurrection*	1900	M.A.	Canon and Sacrist of Rochester Cathedral	Anglican
523 (441)	Pollock, Algernon James	*The Resurrection of the Lord Jesus Christ*	1930?	—	Evangelist	Christian
524 (442)	Porter, Stanley E. et al.	*Resurrection*	1999	Ph.D.	Academic	Christian
525 (443)	Poteat, Edwin McNeill	*These Shared His Power*	1941	Southern Baptist Theological Seminary	Clergyman	Baptist
526 (444)	Power, Philip Bennett	*The Feet of Jesus*	1872	Trinity College	Minister	Anglican
527 (445)	Price, Nelson L.	*The Destruction of Death*	1982	D.D	Pastor	Baptist
528 (445)		*Priceless Pearls for All Christians*	1850			
529 (446)	Priestley, Joseph	*The Evidence of the Resurrection*	1790 [repr. 1794]	Daventry	Minister	Unitarian

530 (447)	Pritchard, John	*Living Easter Through the Year*	2005	Ridley Hall	Bishop	Anglican
531 (448)	Proctor, William	*The Resurrection Report*	1998	Layperson	U.S. Marine Corps Judge Advocate	—
532 (449)	Purves, Andrew	*The Resurrection of Ministry*	2010	Ph.D.	Minister	Presbyterian
533 (450)	Quarles, Charles L.	*Buried Hope or Risen Savior*	2008	Ph.D.	Professor of New Testament and Biblical Theology	Baptist
534 (451)	Quenot, Michel	*The Resurrection and the Icon*	1997	—	Priest	Orthodox
535 (452)	Queripel, John Henry	*On the Third Day*	2018	B.D. and M.Th.	Minister	Protestant
536 (453)	Ramsey, A. Michael	*The Resurrection of Christ: An Essay*	1946	Magdalene College	Archbishop of Canterbury	Anglican
537 (454)	Randolph, B. W.	*The Empty Tomb*	1906	D.D.	Principal of Ely Theological College	Anglican

538 (455)	Rees, Tony	*A Singular Triumph: Jesus Crucified and Risen*	2022	M.A.	Served thirty years in several churches	—
539 (456)	Reeves, Keith Howard	*The Resurrection Narrative in Matthew*	1993	Ph.D.	Professor	Christian
540 (457)	Rex, Helmut. Herbert.	*Did Jesus Rise from the Dead?*	1967	M.A.	Professor of Church History	Presbyterian
541 (458)	Rice, John R.	*The Resurrection of Jesus Christ: Glorious, Heart-Warming Truth*	1953	Did not complete seminary course work	Pastor	Baptist
542 (459)	Richards, Hubert J.	*The First Easter: What Really Happened?*	1986	L.Th. and L.S.S.	Priest	Catholic
543 (460)	Riddle, T. Wilkinson	*The Gospel of the Resurrection: And Other Addresses*	1939	F.R.S.L. and D.P.	Pastor	Baptist
544 (461)	Riga, Peter J.	*The Redeeming Christ*	1969	Ph.D.	Attorney	Catholic
545 (462)	Riggenbach, Eduard	*The Resurrection of Jesus*	1907	College degree	Theologian	Protestant

546 (463)	Riggs, Ollie L.	*Three Days and Three Nights in the Heart of the Earth*	1928	B.A.	Pastor	Baptist
547 (464)	Riley, Gregory J.	*Resurrection Reconsidered*	1995	Ph.D.	Professor of New Testament and Early Christianity	—
548 (465)	Ring, Theophilus Percy	*The Most Certain Fact in History: Addresses on the Resurrection.*	1892	B.A.	Rector	Anglican
549 (466)	Riper, David Van	*The Resurrection of Christ: Reconciling the Gospel Accounts*	2016	Heritage Baptist Institute	Involved in various local church ministries	Christian
550 (467)	Riss, Richard M.	*The Evidence for the Resurrection of Jesus Christ*	1977	Ph.D.	Professor of History	Christian
551 (468)	Roberts, Griffith	*Why We Believe that Christ Rose from the Dead*	1914	Trinity College	Priest	Anglican
552 (469)	Roberts, Robert	*The Trial of the Most Notable Lawsuit of Ancient or Modern Times*	1908	Layperson	Writer	Christadelphian
553 (469)		*Why We Believe that Christ Rose from the Dead*	1914			

554 (470)	Robinette, Brian DuWayne	*Grammars of Resurrection*	2009	Ph.D.	Associate professor	Catholic
555 (471)	Robinson, Charles H.	*Studies in the Resurrection of Christ*	1909	Trinity College	Clergyman	Anglican
556 (472)	Robson, John	*The Resurrection Gospel: A Study of Christ's Great Commission*	1908	D.D.	Missionary	Presbyterian
557 (473)	Rollock, Robert	*Lectures, Upon the History of the Passion, Resurrection, and Ascension*	1616	B.A. and M.A.	Academic	Presbyterian
558 (474)	Roper, Albert L.	*Did Jesus Rise From the Dead? A Lawyer Looks at the Evidence*	1965	University of Virginia	Attorney	Methodist
559 (475)	Roth, Timothy Dean	*The Week that Changed the World: The Complete Easter Story*	2009	B.A.	Adjunct professor of theology	—
560 (476)	Ruch, Velma	*Transformation: A New Creation in Christ*	2006	Ph.D.	Chairperson of the Division of Language and Literature	RLDS Church
561(477)	Runcorn, David	*Rumours of Life: Reflections on the Resurrection Appearances*	1996	—	Vicar	Anglican

562 (478)	Rutland, Mark	*Resurrection: Receiving and Releasing God's Greatest Miracle*	2005	Candler School of Theology	President of Southeastern University	—
563 (479)	Sadler, Ian S.	*The Love of God*	2006	—	Chairman of the Free Grace Evangelistic Association	Baptist
564 (480)	Sancken, Joni S.	*Stumbling Over the Cross: Preaching the Cross and Resurrection Today*	2016	Ph.D.	Associate professor	Mennonite
565 (481)	Sandes, Karl Olav	*Resurrection: Texts and Interpretation*	2020	Ph.D.	Theologian	Christian
566 (482)	Sawicki, Mariann	*Seeing the Lord: Resurrection and Early Christian Practices*	1994	Ph.D.	Educator	Catholic
567 (483)	Sayers, Stanley E.	*He Is Risen*	1990	M.A.	Minister	Church of Christ
568 (484)	Scarborough, Lee Rutland	*After the Resurrection— What?*	1942	Honorary doctorates	Pastor	Southern Baptist
569 (485)	Schlier, Heinrich	*On the Resurrection of Jesus Christ*	2008	Studied Evangelical Theology	Theologian	Catholic

570 (486)	Schneiders, Sandra Marie	*Jesus Risen in Our Midst: Essays on the Resurrection*	2013	S.T.L. and S.T.D.	Professor emerita in the Jesuit School of Theology	Catholic
571 (487)	Schutte, Filip	*Jesus' Resurrection in Joseph's Garden*	2008	Ph.D.	Business coach	Christian
572 (488)	Schwartzkopff, Paul	*The Prophecies of Jesus Christ*	1897	—	Professor of theology	Christian
573 (489)	Schwarzwäller, Klaus	*Cross and Resurrection*	2012	—	Theologian	Christian
574 (490)	Selby, Peter	*Look for the Living*	1976	Ph.D.	Bishop	Anglican
575 (491)	Shafto, George Reginald Holt	*The Reality of the Resurrection*	1930	—	Minister	Anglican
576 (492)	Shaw, John Mackintosh	*The Resurrection of Christ: An Examination*	1920	D.D.	Reverend	Presbyterian
577 (493)	Shepherd, William Henry Jr.	*If a Sermon Falls in the Forest*	2002	Ph.D.	Author	Episcopalian

578 (494)	Sherlock, Thomas	*The Trial of the Witnesses of the Resurrection of Jesus*	1800?	Eton College and St. Catharine's College	Bishop	Anglican
579 (494)		*Proofs of Christianity*	1769			
580 (495)	Silvester, Tipping	*The Evidence of the Resurrection of Jesus Vindicated*	1744	B.A. and M.A.	Divine	Anglican
581 (496)	Simon, Ulrich E.	*The Ascent to Heaven*	1961	—	Deacon	Anglican
582 (497)	Simpson, Albert. B.	*The Christ of the Forty Days*	1890	Theological training	Preacher	Presbyterian
583 (498)	Singleton, Richard O.	*The Last Words of the Resurrected Christ*	1997	—	Reverend	Episcopalian
584 (499)	Sirr, Joseph D' Arcy	*The First Resurrection Considered in a Series of Letters*	1833	D.D.	Rector	Anglican
585 (500)	Skinner, Andrew C.	*The Garden Tomb*	2005	Ph.D.	Dean of religious education	Mormon

586 (501)	Skrine, John Huntley	*Miracle and History*	1912	M.A.	Deacon	Anglican
587 (502)	Slade, Barrett A.	*The Last Week: Atonement and Resurrection*	2020	Ph.D.	Professor of Finance and Real Estate	Church of Later-day Saints
588 (503)	Sleeman, Matthew	*Geography and the Ascension Narrative*	2009	Ph.D.	Reverend	—
589 (504)	Sloan, Harold Paul	*He Is Risen*	1942	D.D.	Minister	Methodist
590 (505)	Smith, Daniel Alan	*Revisiting the Empty Tomb: The Early History of Easter*	2010	Ph.D.	Assistant Professor of New Testament Language and Literature	—
591 (505)		*The Post-Mortem Vindication of Jesus*	2006			
592 (506)	Smith, Graeme	*Was the Tomb Empty? A Lawyer Weighs the Evidence*	2014	—	District Judge of High Court	Methodist
593 (507)	Smith, Robert H.	*Easter Gospels the Resurrection of Jesus*	1963	M.Div., Master of Sacred Theology, and D.Th.	Clergyman	Lutheran

594 (508)	Smith, Stephen H.	*A Sense of Presence: The Resurrection of Jesus in Context*	2016	Ph.D.	Taught religious philosophy	—
595 (509)	Smith, Wilbur M.	*Great Sermons on the Resurrection of Christ*	1964	B.A.	Theologian	Presbyterian
596 (509)		*A Great Certainty in This Hour of World Crisis.*	1951			
597 (510)	Snowden, James Henry	*A Wonderful Morning: An Interpretation of Easter*	1921	D.D.	Adjunct professor of political economy and ethics	Presbyterian
598 (511)	Söderblom, Nathan	*The Death and Resurrection of Christ*	1968	Uppsala University	Archbishop of Uppsala	Church of Sweden
599 (512)	Sparrow-Simpson, W. J.	*The Resurrection and Modern Though*	1915	D.D.	Priest	Anglican
600 (512)		*Our Lord's Resurrection*	1909			
601 (513)	Spencer, Bonnell	*They Saw the Lord*	1947	Williams College	Priest	Episcopalian

602 (514)	Spencer, Claudius B.	*Easter Reflections*	1909	Northwestern University	Pastor	Methodist
603 (515)	Spurgeon, C. H.	*Spurgeon's Sermons on the Death and Resurrection of Jesus*	2005	Layperson	Pastor	Baptist
604 (515)		*Jesus Rose for You*	1998			
605 (515)		*Spurgeon's Sermons on the Resurrection*	1993			
606 (515)		*Twelve Sermons on the Resurrection*	1937			
607 (516)	Stanback, Clarence Foster	*The Resurrection: A Historical Analysis*	2008	Two M.A.s	Chair of the Board of Apologetics Research Society	Christian
608 (517)	Stanford, Charles	*From Calvary to Olivet*	1893	D.D.	Minister	Baptist
609 (518)	Stanford, Shane	*The Seven Next Words of Christ*	2006	Honorary D.D.	Minister	Christian

610 (519)	Stanley, David Michael	*Christ's Resurrection in Pauline Soteriology*	1961	S.J.	Priest	Catholic
611 (520)	Steinmeyer, Franz Ludwig	*The History of the Passion and Resurrection of Our Lord*	1879	—	Professor of theology	Protestant
612 (521)	Stephenson, William	*Days of Joy; Thoughts for all Times*	1955	St. Stanislaus College	Priest	Catholic
613 (521)	Stevenson, Kenneth E., and Gary R. Habermas	*Verdict on the Shroud*	1981	Ph.D.	Pastor	—
614 (522)	Stewart, George	*The Resurrection in Our Street*	1928	Ph.D.	Minister	Presbyterian
615 (523)	Stewart, John J.	*The Eternal Gift: The Story of the Crucifixion and Resurrection.*	1978	M.A.	Associate professor of journalism	Mormon
616 (524)	Stoffel, Ernest Lee	*The Apocalyptic Resurrection of Jesus*	1999	M.Div., Th.M., and Th.D.	Pastor	Presbyterian
617 (525)	Stone, James S.	*The Glory After the Passion*	1913	D.D.	Deacon	Episcopalian

618 (526)	Strobel, Lee	*The Case for the Resurrection*	2009	Honorary D.D.	Author	Christian
619 (526)		*The Case for Easter*	2003			
620 (527)	Sullivan, James	*The Risen Lord*	1963	Theological studies	Auxiliary Bishop	Catholic
621 (528)	Surgy, Paul de., et al.	*The Resurrection and Modern Biblical Thought*	1970	—	Priest	Catholic
622 (529)	Swain, Lionel	*Reading the Easter Gospels*	1993	S.T.L. and L.S.S.	Jerusalem Bible (Nihil Obstat).	Catholic
623 (530)	Swete, Henry Barclay	*The Appearances of Our Lord After the Passion*	1915	D.D.	Deacon	Anglican
624 (530)		*The Ascended Christ*	1911			
625 (531)	Swinburne, Richard	*The Resurrection of God Incarnate*	2003	B.Phil. and theology diploma	Professor of the Philosophy of the Christian Religion	Greek Orthodox

626 (532)	Tait, Arthur J.	*The Heavenly Session of Our Lord*	1912	St. John's College and Ridley Hall	Priest	Anglican
627 (533)	Tatham, C. Ernest	*He Lives: Seven Studies of the Resurrection*	1938	B.A.	Theologian	—
628 (534)	Taylor, John V.	*Weep Not For Me*	1986	Trained for the ministry	Theologian	Anglican
629 (535)	Taylor, Myron J.	*Proclaiming the Risen Lord*	2006	Honorary D.D.	Educator	Christian
630 (536)	Tenney, Merrill C.	*The Reality of the Resurrection*	1963	Ph.D.	Pastor	Christian
631 (537)		*Resurrection Realities: "Now is Christ Risen"*	1945			
632 (538)	Thatcher, Floyd W.	*The Gift of Easter*	1976	—	Vice President of Word Books Publisher	—
633 (539)	Thayer, Erastus William	*The Bloody Sacrifice*	1898	D.D.	Pastor	Presbyterian

634 (540)	Theisz, George Elmer	The Eight First Words of the Risen Saviour	1950			—
635 (541)	Thomas, George Ernest	The Meaning of the Resurrection	1964	B.R.E., S.T.B., and Th.D.	Elder	Methodist
636 (542)	Thompson, Alan J.	The Acts of the Risen Lord Jesus	2011	Ph.D.	Head of the New Testament department	Christian
637 (543)	Thompson, Alexander P.	Recognition and the Resurrection Appearances of Luke 24	2023	Ph.D.	Pastor	Methodist
638 (544)	Thompson, Gordon G.	Living the Easter Faith	2004	M.Div.	Pastor	Methodist
639(545)	Thompson, K. C.	Received Up Into Glory	1964	M.A.	Deacon	Anglican
640 (546)	Thomson, Alexander	Did Jesus Rise from the Dead?	1940			—
641 (547)	Thorburn, Thomas James	The Resurrection Narratives and Modern Criticism	1910	D.D.	Clerk in Holy Orders	Anglican

642 (548)	Thorogood, Bernard	*Risen Today*	1986	D.D.	Minister	United Reformed Church
643 (549)	Toon, Peter	*The Ascension of Our Lord*	1984	B.D. and D.Phil.	Deacon	Anglican
644 (550)	Torrance, Thomas F.	*Space, Time, and Resurrection*	1976	Ph.D.	Priest	Presbyterian
645 (551)	Torrey, R. A.	*Is the Bible the Inerrant Word of God*	1922	Yale University and Yale Divinity School	Evangelist	Protestant
646 (552)	Tóth, Tihamér	*The Risen Christ: Sermons on the Resurrection*	1938	Doctoral degree	Priest	Catholic
647 (553)	Townson, Thomas	*A Discourse on the Evangelical History*	1793	D.D.	Archdeacon of Richmond	Anglican
648 (554)	Trench, George Henry	*The Crucifixion and Resurrection of Christ by the Light of Tradition*	1908	B.A.	Writer	—
649 (555)	Trull, Joe E.	*The Seven Last Words of the Risen Christ*	1985	Th.D.	Pastor	Christian

650 (556)	Trumper, Peter R.G.	*Breakfast on the Beach*	1999	Aberystwyth Theological College	Pastor	Protestant
651 (557)	Tulga, Chester Earl.	*The Case for the Resurrection of Jesus Christ*	1951	—	Clergyman	Baptist
652 (558)	Upham, Francis W.	*The First Words from God*	1894	B.A.	Educator	—
653 (559)	van Daalen, David H.	*The Real Resurrection*	1972	—	Minister	Presbyterian
654 (560)	Vander, Ray Laan	*Death and Resurrection of the Messiah*	2009	M.Div.	Founder of That the World May Know Ministries	Christian
655 (561)	Varley, Henry	*The Evangel of the Risen Christ*	1901	No formal education	Evangelist	Christian Reformed Church
656 (561)	Verheyden, Joseph et al.	*'If Christ has not been raised ...'*	2016	Three M.A.s and STD	Professor	Catholic
657 (562)	Vinzent, Markus	*Christ's Resurrection in Early Christianity*	2011	Ph.D.	Religious historian	—

658 (563)	Violette, Ebal Eleadah	*In Palestine at the Empty Tomb*	1923	Northern Prairie Seminary	Clergyman	Christ Disciples Church
659 (564)	Vistar, Deolito V.	*The Cross-and-Resurrection*	—	Ph.D.	Pastor	Christian
660 (565)	Wace, Henry	*The Story of the Resurrection*	1923	D.D.	Curacies	Anglican
661 (566)	Wade, George	*Two Discourses: The First, an Appeal to the Miracles of Jesus as Proofs of His Messiahship*	1729	D.D.	Deacon	Anglican
662 (567)	Walker, Peter W. L.	*The Weekend That Changed the World*	2000	Research fellow	Minister	Anglican
663 (568)	Wallace, J. Warner	*Alive: A Cold-Case Approach to the Resurrection*	2014	Two M.As	Homicide detective	Christian
664 (569)	Wansbrough, Henry	*Risen From the Dead*	1978	OSB., MA STL., and LSS.	Biblical scholar	Catholic
665 (569)		*The Resurrection*	1975			

666 (570)	Ward, Nelson W.	*"The Master Key"* . . . *to the* *Problems of* *Passion Week*	1915	Layperson	U.S. Army Medal of Honor recipient (Civil War)	—
667 (571)	Warnock, Adrian	*Raised with Christ*	2010	M.D.	Medical doctor	—
668 (572)	Warren, Elizabeth Whately	*The Great Forty Days Following the Resurrection*	1876	Layperson	—	
669 (573)	Water, Mark	*Understanding the Resurrection*	2004	London College of Divinity	Trained for the ministry	Anglican
670 (574)	Waterman, Mark Masataka Watanabe	*The Empty Tomb Tradition of Mark*	2006	Ph.D.	Born in Japan.	—
671 (575)	Watson, John Ian MacLaren	*Children of the Resurrection*	1912	D.D.	Minister	Free Church of Scotland
672 (576)	Watson, Nigel M.,	*The Heart of the Matter*	1980	Ph.D.	Professor of the New Testament	Presbyterian

673 (577)	Weatherhead, Leslie Dixon	*The Manner of the Resurrection in the Light of Modern Science*	1959	Richmond Theological College	Pastor	Methodist
674 (577)		*The Resurrection of Christ in the Light of Modern Science*	1959			
675 (577)		*The Resurrection and the Life*	1953			
676 (578)	Weaver, Jonathan	*Discourses on the Resurrection*	1871	D.D.	Bishop	Protestant
677 (579)	Webb, Guilford Polly	*Jesus on Trial To Day*	1914	Savoy College	Attorney	Christian
678 (580)	Wedderburn, A. J. M.	*Beyond Resurrection*	1999	D.Phil.	Theology educator	Reformed
679 (581)	Wenham, John William	*Easter Enigma*	1993	M.A.	Priest	Anglican
680 (582)	Weren, W.J.C., H. Van De Sandt, and J. Verheyden,	*Life Beyond the Death in Matthew's Gospel*	2011	Ph.D.	Professor Emeritus of Biblical Studies	—

681(583)	West, Gilbert	*Observations on the History and Evidences of the Resurrection*	1749	B.A.	Poet	Christian
682 (583)	West, Gilbert	*A Defence of the Christian Revelation*	1748	B.A.	Poet	Christian
683 (584)	West, John Rowland	*Parish Sermons on the Ascension*	1871	A.B. and A.M.	Vicar	Anglican
684 (585)	Westcott, Brooke Foss	*The Gospel of the Resurrection*	1891	B.A., honorary degrees	Lord Bishop of Durham	Anglican
685 (586)	Whatmore, Leonard Elliott.	*The Resurrection Under Attack*	1979	M.A.	Parish priest	Catholic
686 (587)	White, Bill W.L.	*Risen Indeed: Six Weeks That Changed the World*	1993	—	Pastor	—

687 (588)	White, Ellen Gould Harmon	*Message from Calvary: The Day God Died for You*	1981 (reprint)	No formal education	Co-founder of the Seventh-day Adventist Church	Seventh-day Adventist
688 (588)		*The Great Controversy Between Christ and Satan*	1878			
689 (588)		*Redemption: or the Resurrection of Christ*	1877			
690 (589)	Whiton, James Morris	*The Gospel of the Resurrection*	1881	Ph.D.	Pastor	Congregational
691 (590)	Wiebe, Phillip H.	*Visions of Jesus: Direct Encounters*	1997	Ph.D.	Chair of the Department of Philosophy	—
692 (591)	Wiersbe, Warren W.	Wiersbe, Warren W., comp. *Classic Sermons on the Resurrection*	1991	Bachelor of Theology	Pastor	Christian
693 (592)	Wilckens, Ulrich	*Resurrection: Biblical Testimony*	1978	Studied Protestant theology	Professor of New Testament	Lutheran

694 (593)	Williams, Isaac	*Our Lord's Resurrection*	1904	D.D.	Deacon	Anglican
694 (593)		*The Gospel Narrative of Our Lord's Resurrection*	1855			
695 (594)	Williams, Norman Powell	*The First Easter Morning: A Suggested Harmony*	1920	Christ Church	Theologian	Anglican
696 (595)	Williams, Rowan	*Resurrection: Interpreting the Easter Gospel*	1982	D.Phil.	Archbishop of Canterbury	Anglican
697 (596)	Wilson, William	*A Discourse of the Resurrection*	1694	M.A.	Archdeacon of Coventry	Anglican
698 (597)	Wingeier, Douglas E	*Jesus Christ: Resurrection*	1985	Ph.D.	Pastor	Methodist
699 (598)	Wise, Robert L	*The Son Rises: Resurrecting the Resurrection*	2008	Ph.D.	Archbishop	Methodist
700 (599)	Witcher, Walter Campbell	*Legal Proof: Being an Answer to Thomas H. Huxley*	1937	Layperson	Lawyer	Christian

701 (600)	Wolfe, Charles E.	*The Post Resurrection Appearances: A Commentary*	1988	—	Pastor	Methodist
702 (601)	Wolfe, Rolland E.	*How the Easter Story Grew from Gospel to Gospel*	1989	Ph.D.	Professor at Tufts	—
703 (602)	Wood, William (of Lexington)	*The Antichrist Identified*	1918	—	Lawyer	—
704 (603)	Woodington, J. David	*The Dubious Disciples*	2020	Ph.D.	Academic advisor	—
705 (604)	Woodrow, Ralph Edward	*Three Days and Three Nights: Reconsidered in Light of Scripture*	1993	—	Minister	Christian
706 (605)	Wright, N. T.	*The Challenge of Easter*	2009	D. Phil.	Bishop of Durham	Anglican
707 (605)		*The Resurrection of the Son of God*	2003			
708 (605)	Wright, N.T., and John Dominic Crossan	*The Resurrection of Jesus*	2006	D. Phil	—	

709 (606)	Wuellner, Bernard	*Graces of the Risen Christ*	1960	S.J.	Priest	Catholic
710 (607)	Yarnold, Greville Dennis	*Risen Indeed: Studies in the Lord's Resurrection*	1959	M.A.	Warden of St Deiniol's Library	—
711 (608)	Yarrington, William Henry Hazell	*The Resurrection of Jesus Christ and Kindred Subjects*	1910–1919	M.A.	Deacon	Anglican
712 (609)	Zwemer, Samuel Marinus	*The Glory of the Empty Tomb*	1947	D.D.	Missionary	Reformed Church
713 (610)	Zwiep, Arie W.	*The Ascension of the Messiah in Lukan Christology*	1997	Ph.D.	Professor of Hermeneutics	Christian

Table 4: Contra Resurrection Authors and Texts

Book (Author) #	Author Name	Text	Year	Degree(s)	Occupation	Religion
1 (1)	Ahmad, Mirza Ghulam	*Masih Hindustan Mein* (*Jesus in India*)	1899	Education in Arabic, Persian, Qur'an, and medicine	Indian religious leader	Muslim
2 (2)	Allen, Don [pseud.]. Hiram L. True	The *Resurrection* of Jesus: *An Agnostic's View*	1893	M.D.	American physician	—
3 (3)	Alter, Michael J.	*The Resurrection and Its Apologetics: Jesus' Death and Burial*	2023 (forthcoming)	M.S.	American teacher	Jewish
4 (3)		*A Thematic Access-Oriented Bibliography of Jesus's Resurrection*	2020			
5 (3)		*The Resurrection: A Critical Inquiry*	2015			

6 (4)	Annet, Peter	*Supernaturals Examined: In Four Dissertations on Three Treatises*	1750	Little formal education	Schoolmaster	Deist and early freethinker
7 (4)		*The Resurrection of Jesus Demonstrated to Have No Proof*	1745			
8 (4)		*The Resurrection Defenders Stript of All Defence*	1744			
9 (4)		*The Resurrection of Jesus Considered in Answer to the Trial of the Witnesses*	1744			
10 (4)		*The Resurrection Reconsidered: Being an Answer to the Clearer and Others*	1744			
11 (5)	Aus, Roger	*The Death, Burial and Resurrection of Jesus, and Death, Burial, and Translation of Moses in Judaic Tradition*	2008	Ph.D.	Pastor	Lutheran
12 (6)	Austin, Benjamin Fish	*The Crucifixion and The Resurrection of Jesus by an Eye-Witness*	1919	B.D. and D.D.	Canadian educator	Former Methodist
13 (7)	Bell, William S.	*The Resurrection of Jesus*	1910	—	Minister and Preacher	Freethinker

14 (8)	Berna, Kurt (pseud for John Reban and Hans Nabe)	*A World Discovery: Christ Did Not Perish on the Cross*	1975	—	Author	Catholic
15 (8)		*Inquest on Jesus Christ*	1967			
16 (9)	Clarke, John A.	*A Critical Review of the Life, Character, Miracles, and Resurrection of Jesus Christ*	1839	None	Bookshop Clerk	Former Methodist
17 (10)	Connor, Robert P.	*Apparitions of Jesus: The Resurrection as Ghost Story*	2018	Western Kentucky University	—	
18 (11)	Covington, Nicholas Ryan	*Extraordinary Claims, Extraordinary Evidence, and the Resurrection of Jesus*	2012	—	Author	—
19 (12)	Crossan, John Dominic and N. T. Wright.	*The Resurrection of Jesus: John Dominic Crossan and N. T. Wright in Dialogue*	2006	S.T.D. and D.D.	Professors	Former Catholic Priest; Apologist
20 (12)	Crossan, John Dominic and William Lane Craig.	*Will the Real Jesus Please Stand Up?*	1998	D.D.; Ph.D.		
21 (13)	Derrett, J. Duncan M.	*The Anastasis: The Resurrection of Jesus as an Historical Event*	1982	D.C.L., Ph.D., and LLD.	Professor of Oriental Laws in the University of London	—

22 (14)	Docker, Ernest Brougham	*If Jesus Did Not Die on the Cross: A Study in Evidence*	1920	M.A.	Australian District Court Judge	Anglican
23 (15)	Furneaux, Rupert	*The Empty Tomb: The World's Greatest Mystery*	1963	Educated at Eastbourne College	British writer	—
24 (16)	Gorham, Charles Turner	*The First Easter Dawn*	1908	Educated privately	Co-founder, Rationalist Press Association	Rationalist
25 (17)	Hallquist, Chris	*UFOs, Ghosts, and a Rising God*	2009	M.A	—	Atheist
26 (18)	Hanhart, Karel	*The Open Tomb: A New Approach*	1995	M.Div. and D. Min.	Dutch Presbyterian pastor	Presbyterian
27 (19)	Hegemann, Werner	*Christ Rescued*	1933	Ph.D. (Economics)	German city planner	Evangelical
28 (20)	Jacobovci, Simcha	*The Jesus Family Tomb*	2007	M.A.	Canadian film director	Jewish
29 (21)	Kent, Jack A.	*The Psychological Origins of the Resurrection Myth*	1999	M.Div.	Minister	Unitarian

30 (22)	Kersten, Holger	*The Jesus Conspiracy: The Turin Shroud and the Truth About the Resurrection*	1994	Studied theology and pedagogy	German writer	Protestant
31 (22)		*Jesus Lived in India: His Unknown Life*	1994			
32 (23)	Jacobs, Alan	*Jesus Lived in India*	2009	—	Student of mysticism	—
33 (24)	Komarnitsky, Kris D.	*Doubting Jesus' Resurrection: What Happened in the Black Box?*	2014	—	Aviation	Rationalist
34 (25)	Lüdemann, Gerd	*The Resurrection of Christ: A Historical Inquiry*	2004	Ph.D.	German biblical scholar	Atheist
35 (25)		*What Happened to Jesus: A Historical Approach to the Resurrection*	1995			
36 (25)		*The Resurrection of Jesus: History, Experience, Theology*	1994			
37 (26)	McCabe, Joseph	*The Myth of the Resurrection*	1925	Catholic University of Louvain	Former Priest	Atheist

No.	Author	Title	Year	Education	Occupation	Religion
38 (27)	Mirsch, David	*The Open Tomb: Why and Why Jesus Faked His Death and Resurrection*	2011	—		
39 (28)	Nickell, Joe	*Inquest on the Shroud of Turin*	1983	Ph.D.	Committee for Skeptical Inquiry	—
40 (29)	Notovitch, Nicolas	*The Unknown Life of Jesus Christ*	1894	—	Adventurer	Jewish
41 (30)	Pearce, Jonathan M.S.	*The Resurrection: A Critical Examination of the Easter Story*	2021	Masters in Philosophy, University of Leeds	Teacher	Atheist
42 (31)	Price, Robert M.	*Night of the Living Saviour*	2011	Ph.D. (Systematic Theology); Ph.D. (New Testament)	Author	Self-declared Christian Atheist
43 (31)		*Jesus is Dead*	2007			
44 (31)		*The Empty Tomb: Jesus Beyond the Grave*	2005			
45 (32)	Prokofieff, Sergei O.	*The Mystery of the Resurrection in the Light of Anthroposophy*	2010	—	Russian anthroposophy	—

46 (33)	Rhys, Jocelyn	*Shaken Creeds: The Resurrection Doctrines*	1924	—		
47 (34)	Ross, William Stewart	*Did Jesus Rise from the Dead?*	1887	Studied at Glasgow University	Author	Secularist
48 (35)	Sandoval, Chris	*Can Christians Prove the Resurrection: A Reply to Apologists*	2010	M.S.	ǀ	
49 (36)	Schonfield, Hugh J.	*After the Cross*	1981	Doctor of Sacred Literature	Biblical Scholar	Secular Jew
50 (36)		*The Passover Plot*	1966			
51 (37)	Scott, Bernard Brandon	*The Trouble With the resurrection From Paul to the Fourth Gospel*	2010	Ph.D.	Professor of New Testament	Catholic
52 (37)		*The Resurrection of Jesus: A Source Book*	2009			
53 (38)	Sheehan, Thomas	*The First Coming: How the Kingdom of God Became Christianity*	1986	Ph.D.	American philosopher	Non-conformist

54 (39)	Sigal, Gerald	*The Resurrection Fantasy: Reinventing Jesus*	2012	M.S.	American educator	Jewish
55 (40)	Simmons, Graham	*Jesus After the Crucifixion*	2007	—	Archeologist	—
56 (41)	Spong, John Shelby	*Resurrection: Myth or Reality?*	1994	M.Div., honorary D.D.s, honorary Doctor of Humane Letters	Bishop	Episcopalian
57 (41)		*The Easter Movement*	1980			
58 (42)	Strecher, Carl and Craig L. Bomberg	*Resurrection: Faith or Fact?*	2019	Ph.D.	Professor of English	Atheist
59 (43)	Thiering, Barbara	*Jesus & the Riddle of the Dead Sea Scrolls*	1992	Ph.D.	Australian historian	—
60 (44)	Twyman, Tracy R.	*The Jesus Goat: The Substitution Theory of the Crucifixion*	2011	—	Podcast producer	—
61 (45)	Wolfe, Rolland	*How the Easter Story Grew from Gospel to Gospel*	1989	—	Biblical scholar	Christian

62 (46)	Yusef, Abdulbaset	*Jesus: From India to Japan*	2017	M.D.	Internist	Muslim

Conclusion

Actress Clara Pelle asked the famous question, "Where's the beef?" In theology, the question that requires answering is where is the beef supporting Habermas's claims? It requires remembering that Gary Habermas's publications report that he has identified roughly 3,400 resurrection sources. Moreover, he elaborated that they were (1) published from 1975 to 2010; (2) books and journal articles; and (3) in English, French, and German. His research found that a 3:1 ratio (75%) of scholars accepted the empty tomb, and an even higher percentage endorsed other minimal facts about the resurrection. Looking at the data another way, Habermas is saying that at least 25 percent of authors or scholars reject the empty tomb as a fact. In contrast, research by Alter differs from that of Habermas in several ways. His investigation incorporated (1) exclusively nonjuvenile English-language materials; (2) texts at least forty-eight pages; and (3) books written in the past five centuries.

This investigation analyzed approximately 775 texts (including six double-counted debates), with 713 pros and 62 contras. Pro authors were 610 and forty-six contras. The data substantiates and expands the earlier report by Alter and Slade. This article provides evidence that a remarkably high proportion of the English-language books written about Jesus' resurrection were by members of the clergy or people linked to seminaries and those having a professional and personal interest in the subject matter.

Material from the Alter and Slade article bears repeating:

A remarkably high proportion of the books written about Jesus' resurrection were by members of the clergy or people linked to seminaries, which means any so-called scholarly consensus on the subject of Jesus' resurrection is wildly inflated due to a biased sample of authors who have a professional and personal interest in the subject matter. No doubt that the same holds true for journal article publications, as well. *Pro-Resurrection authors outnumber Contra-Resurrection authors by a factor of about twelve-to-one.* (Italics for emphasis)

This investigation substantiates assertions that Christians of various denominations write the vast majority of texts published on Jesus' resurrection. This review determined that virtually all of the Pro-Resurrection Christian authors are, in fact, "true believers" with pre-critical and occupational biases in favor of orthodox Christian dogma. A literature review of the source confirms that many of the authors are apologists, evangelists, ministers, priests, or administrators and professors in theological seminaries and universities. Consequently, the vast majority likely have a vested interest in the outcome of their research, something Habermas himself warns against.

By now, the flaw in the second criterion listed in Habermas's 2005 and 2012 articles should be apparent to the reader. Habermas's numbers merely expose the likelihood of a confirmation bias among credentialed "true believers" who conclude something that they already believed to begin with: Jesus raised from the dead. The data that Habermas has amassed is not proportionately pulled from all relevant subclasses of critical scholarship and is, therefore, unrepresentative of the actual historio-theological landscape. The data Habermas has gathered is not only tainted by virtue of his own professional biases (data gathered by advocacy groups like Christian apologetic institutions.

The data in this article provides evidentiary proof that most authors of pro-resurrection texts have a vested interest in the outcome. Returning to Alter and Slade,

That said, this article does not wish to assert that a Christian scholar cannot write an objective and critical text on the topic of Jesus' resurrection. Indeed, a literature review found that several detractors were once Christians, and some were former "believers" who later deconverted. Conversely, a review of the literature shows that some non-Christians and marginal Christians alike have converted or become stronger believers ("more mature in their faith") in Christianity after a deeper inquiry into the subject.[33]

---

[33] Alter and Slade, "Dataset Analysis," 385.

Clara Pelle was correct to inquire angrily, "Where's the beef?" Biblical scholars, theologians, and detractors are equally spot-on when they indigently ask Habermas to provide his evidence. For almost twenty years, they have made requests to examine the data. This article provides beef and kosher at that.

BIBLIOGRAPHY

Alter, Michael J. *The Resurrection and Its Apologetics: Jesus' Death and Burial Vol. 1.* Denver: GCRR, (forthcoming).

———. *A Thematic Access-Oriented Bibliography of Jesus's Resurrection.* Eugene, OR: Resource Publications, 2020.

Alter, Michael J., and Darren M. Slade. "Dataset Analysis of English Texts Written on the Topic of Jesus' Resurrection: A Statistical Critique of Minimal Facts Apologetics." *SHERM* 3 no. 2, (2021): 367–392.

Carrier, Richard. "Innumeracy: A Fault to Fix." *Richard Carrier Blogs*, November 26, 2013. https://tinyurl.com/2uuj52ss

Dembski, William A., and Mike Licona, eds. *Evidence for GOD: 50 Arguments for Faith from the Bible, History, Philosophy, and Science.* Baker Books, 2010.

"Doctor of Divinity." *Wikipedia*, May 8, 2023. https://tinyurl.com/4z8tshxs

Ehrman, Bart D. *"Can Biblical Scholars Be Historians?"* The Bart Ehrman Blog, (blog), January 13, 2017. https://tinyurl.com/4pt2stc2

Frame, John M. A Presuppositionalist's Response [to Evidential Apologetics]." In Five Views on Apologetics, edited by Stanley N. Gundry and Steven B. Cowan. Counterpoints: Bible and Theology, 132-37. Grand Rapids: Zondervan, 2000.

Habermas, Gary R. "APOL 900: Historical Jesus PhD Intensive." Lecture, Liberty University - Liberty Mountain Conference Room 103, Lynchburg, VA, May 23–27, 2016.

———. "The Minimal Facts Approach to the Resurrection of Jesus: The Role of Methodology as a Crucial Component in Establishing Historicity.*" Southern Theological* Review 3, no. 1 (2012): 15–26.

———. *On the Resurrection, Volume 1: Evidences.* Nashville: B&H Academic, 2024.

———. "Resurrection Research from 1975 to the Present: What Are Critical Scholars Saying?" *Journal for the Study of the Historical Jesus* 3, no. 2 (2005): 135–53. https://tinyurl.com/zax8x4j7

Habermas, Gary R. and Michael R. Licona: *The Case for the Resurrection of Jesus.* Grand Rapids: Kregel, 2004.

Koukl, Gregory. *Tactics: A Game Plan for Discussing Your Christian Convictions.* Grand Rapids: Zondervan, 2009.

Licona, Michael R. *The Resurrection of Jesus: A New Historiographical Approach.* Downers Grove, IL: IVP Academic, 2010.

Loke, Andrew. *Investigating the Resurrection of Jesus Christ: A New Transdisciplinary Approach.* New York: Routledge, 2020.

McGrew, Lydia. "About Me," May 14, 2021. https://tinyurl.com/5n7un94d

McLaren, Brian D., and Tony Campolo. *Adventures in Missing the Point: How the Culture-Controlled Church Neutered the Gospel.* Grand Rapids, MI: Zondervan, 2003.

Minton, Evan. "The Concept of the Credentialed Layman - Cerebral Faith." Cerebral Faith – Christian Apologetics, Biblical Studies, Systematic Theology, an Intellectually Fulfilled Christianity, January 12, 2023. https://tinyurl.com/2v8f5uuw

Morley, Brian K. *Mapping Apologetics: Comparing Contemporary Approaches.* Downers Grove, IL: IVP Academic, 2015.

Richardsh. "25 August 1975 Pinchas Lapide and Hans Kung Dialogue #otdimjh." On This Day In Messianic Jewish History, August 25, 2015. https://jewinthepew.org/2015/08/25/25-august-1975-pinchas-lapide-and-hans-kung-dialogue-otdimjh/.

Shaw, Benjamin C.F. "Philosophy of History, Historical Jesus Studies, and Miracles: Three Roadblocks to Resurrection Research." PhD diss. Liberty University, 2021.

Stewart, Robert B. "On Habermas's Minimal Facts Argument." In *Raised on the Third Day: Defending the Historicity of the Resurrection of Jesus,* edited by W. David Beck and Michael R Licona, 1–14. Bellingham: Lexham Press, 2020.

ABOUT THE AUTHOR

Michael J. Alter taught in the Miami-Dade County Public School System for over forty years. He published *The Name Israel* (2023) and *A Thematic Access-Oriented Bibliography of Jesus's Resurrection* with Resource Publications (2020). His 602-page text identified approximately 7,000 English-language sources from books on that subject. Five years earlier, he penned *The Resurrection: A Critical Inquiry* (2015) and has assisted in editing several other texts. Alter has also published with Jason Aronson, *Why the Torah Begins with the Letter Beit* (1998) and *What Is The Purpose Of Creation? A Jewish Anthology* (1991). Both books were the main selection of "The Jewish Book Club." Forthcoming is *The Resurrection and Its Apologetics: Jesus' Death and Burial.*

MORE FROM THE AUTHOR

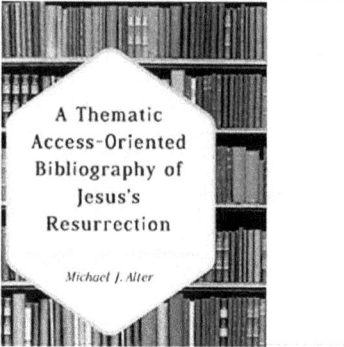

*Thematic Access-Oriented
Bibliography of Jesus's
Resurrection*
source Publications, 2020

Xlibris, 2015

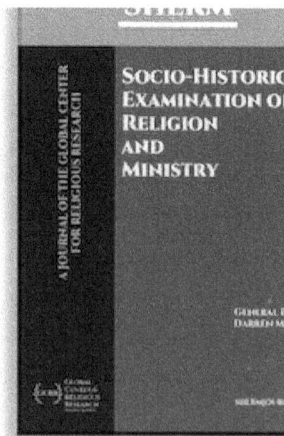